WITHDRAWN

FV

635 S848d
STEVENSON
DOWN-TO-EARTH GARDENING
                    6.98

St. Louis Community College

Library

5801 Wilson Avenue
St. Louis, Missouri 63110

VIOLET STEVENSON

Down-to-earth Gardening

HAMLYN

LONDON·NEW YORK·SYDNEY·TORONTO

We would like to thank Pat Brindley
and the Harry Smith Horticultural Photographic Collection
for the colour photographs used in this book.

Line Drawings by Ron Hayward

First published in paperback form in 1967
Revised and published in hardback form in 1975 by
The Hamlyn Publishing Group Limited
London · New York · Sydney · Toronto
Astronaut House, Feltham, Middlesex, England

Filmset in 10 on 11½ pt Monophoto Sabon by
Tradespools Ltd, Frome, Somerset

Printed and bound in England by
Chapel River Press, Andover, Hampshire

ISBN 0 600 32903 8

Contents

Introduction

For as long as I can remember I have been a gardener. One of the most famous men in British horticulture passed me for my Girl Guide gardening badge when I was twelve and since then the top gardeners in several lands have been my friends and my tutors. Most of my life I have had a large garden in which to practice all I have learned, but on the other hand for brief periods pots and window-boxes have been the extent of my plot.

Twenty years or so ago I began to put down on paper the results of some of my experiences, the joys and the agonies of gardening, the problems I have encountered and how I have overcome them, the tips gleaned from experienced men and women which have helped me, and not all of them so-called experts. In these twenty years I have had a voluminous correspondence with gardeners all over the world, an invaluable aid in teaching me the hopes, the problems, the pleasures and the worries of the millions of people who enjoy gardening as the greatest of all hobbies.

I have learned and I have been taught many short cuts. I have found out that if the correct way involves too much time, labour or expense, then there will be a quicker, an easier and a cheaper way.

All of this has given me confidence to feel that I have something worth passing on. And the thought that I would most like to pass on to readers is that in your gardens you are the boss. *You* decide what kind of a garden you would like; the garden does not decide for itself. *You* decide what plants to grow. *You* decide how much time you can afford to spend in the garden. Whether your plot is already a green and pleasant land or rank wilderness, whether the area to be cultivated is large or small, whether your available time and energy is such that you can encompass acres of horticultural wealth or whether through other ties or perhaps age or infirmity your gardening is confined to a few pot plants makes no difference. *You* should be the boss, never the slave.

Once this simple fact has been accepted, the puzzles, the fears and the complexities of gardening seem to lose their importance. For if *you* are in command you must win.

The easier we make our gardening the more we will enjoy it. I am a busy woman with a large garden, a family to mother, a great deal of travelling to do and a job to fulfil and enjoy. I have found it necessary in all of these to find the easiest, quickest and cheapest way to carry out my inevitable tasks. And this has given me the leisure and the energy to enjoy my life to its fullest.

If, with this book, I have been able to show you just how easy gardening can be, then my own pleasure in writing it will have been increased.   v.s.

Soil

Everything in the garden depends on the soil. If you co-operate with your soil right from the beginning, you will find it a wonderful ally which will repay with vast interest the modest efforts you put into it. And fortunately, practically all soils will grow some plants, so if you choose those that grow best on your soil half your work will be done for you. On the other hand, if you have a passion for certain types of plants which do not take kindly to your particular soil, it is still possible to grow them if you make special preparations.

Obviously, the first thing to do is to find out what kind of soil you have. Soils can be acid or alkaline and sections of the garden can, in some instances, differ radically from each other in their composition and their chemical content. At one end of the scale we have soils which are all peat – acid – and at the other end those which are chalk – non-acid or alkaline. Usually a glance at neighbours' gardens will give you a quick clue. If rhododendrons abound, then you are on acid soil. If clematis and lavender grow well, or wallflowers and stocks shine in their glory, then there is lime about. If you are still uncertain, have a word with the local nurseryman. However, you may need to know more than a casual glance can reveal.

One kind of soil has to end somewhere and another begin, and it is as likely to be in your plot that this transition takes place as any other. Again, continuous cultivation tends to increase the acidity of a soil, so where one section has been cultivated and another has not there will be differences.

Soils can be light, heavy or medium in texture, and this is repeated in actual weight so that a heavy soil is much harder to work. It is easy enough to tell whether soil is light and sandy, heavy, clayey, or chalky, but it is also more simple than perhaps you realise to make a rough test of acidity or alkalinity.

One way to do this is to buy a packet of litmus papers from the chemist or the garden shop and test with these on a well-shaken-up mixture of soil and water. (If you take soil samples – a trowelful is a good amount – from more than one area, and test them separately you will get a clearer picture of your garden soil.)

Acid soils turn blue litmus paper pink and limy soils turn pink litmus paper blue. But this is a very elementary test. You can buy soil testing kits quite cheaply which will give you much more

detail. Furthermore, many garden chemists and horticultural societies will test your soil if you submit samples.

While you are doing this carry the experiment further. Put a handful of soil in a clear drinking glass half full of water and stir well. Allow it to settle for a few minutes, and you will have a helpful clue to the composition of your soil. Sand and gravel will sink immediately to the bottom, good loam and clay will look like a muddy suspension in the solution. The all-important humus, about which more later, will float on the top. Your aim should be for a fairly equal proportion of all three. Where one or more is missing, you will have to treat your garden soil to obtain the correct balance.

But to return to the question of content in the soil. As you can see, it is essential that we have some kind of measure for acidity and alkalinity so that we can describe the type of soil we have. These factors are measured on what is known as the pH scale. The neutral measurement is pH 7·0. Above this soils are alkaline, and below this they are acid and they should be treated accordingly.

Most garden soils are round about this figure (usually between pH 6·0 and pH 8·0). However, most of the plants we like to cultivate enjoy a slightly acid soil with a pH of about 6·5. So we should try to get a little acidity into our soils. This is difficult to maintain on limy and chalky soils because rain water is constantly washing more lime into the soil, but one can persevere by adding peat, leafmould, grass cuttings and other humus-forming materials, all of which tend to make the soil acid in time. It may help if you remember that peat is composed entirely of humus, with very little chalk or lime or none at all. Soil is ground or powdered rock. Where you are on limestone or surrounded by it your soil is bound to be limy although it may be dark in colour and not white like chalky soil.

There is now a chemical called Sequestrene which helps acid-loving plants growing in soils that tend to become limy. I use this on magnolias, rhododendrons, and other calcifuges (the term given to plants that cannot tolerate lime) to keep them in good health. Sequestrene contains chelated iron which is essential to plants and which acid lovers cannot get in limy soils. It acts rather as an iron tonic does to some of us whose blood is deficient in that mineral. It is fairly expensive, but only very little is necessary and one dose a year is usually sufficient unless a plant is suffering badly. Its absorption is almost miraculous. I have seen the leaf colour of a magnolia change from green-yellow – indicative of too much lime – to deep green, in twenty-four hours.

The best way to get soil into condition so that it can benefit from your administrations is to dig it well. If this is not skimped at the beginning, then when your permanent plants are established their roots will be well nourished.

Many people accept the fact that fertilisers and manures are needed for plant growth, but do not seem to be aware that air in the soil is also essential.

A well-cultivated soil has plenty of air spaces between the soil particles. When it's watered, the water should rush through it and fill these spaces, driving out the stale air and dragging fresh air after it. As the plants take up the water, more air enters the soil and re-occupies the spaces. Without this continual cycle, soils become heavy, roots become drowned and plants die.

Some soils drain too rapidly (sandy and light soils are examples), the plant foods become lost and so the soil becomes poor. In this case we must restrain the rapid rush of water by incorporating body or humus. To improve soil of this kind add well-rotted manure, home-made compost, rotted straw and grass mowings either on the surface as mulches or dug in, preferably both.

In heavy soils the water cannot rush through nor can the air penetrate. Much the same materials are added but this time for lightening purposes. Also to lighten the texture of the soil, coarse, well-washed or weathered ashes (those taken straight from the grate contain too much sulphur), sharp sand and peat may be incorporated.

Sometimes soils, particularly clay types, are waterlogged and this can be so bad that drainage pipes or soakaways must be provided. A sure sign that soil is waterlogged can be seen after a heavy rainfall where the water hangs about in one area when it has disappeared elsewhere. This is most often to be found on new estates where the area has been badly panned while building was in progress. It is also found on lawns where the grass has been sown or laid on soil not properly prepared. In bad cases the cure must be drastic. Either re-lay a lawn or install a drainage system which will take surplus water away. Sometimes aeration of the lawn by spiking will relieve the trouble.

One of the best ways to improve any soil is to dig animal manure into it. I know that this is not so easily found but a search for stables or a farm which will provide it is well worthwhile. Cow dung is best for light soils, and horse or stable manure best for heavy ones. For thin, poor and chalky or sandy soils which have no humus at all, heavy pig manure is best.

None of these manures should be used in a fresh state when they can be harmful. Make certain they are well rotted. If you cannot buy rotted manures, stack fresh ones in the 'dry', by covering the heap with polythene. Try to make it roughly square shaped so that it will take less room. It is also a good idea to scoop out the ground a little beforehand and line the depression with polythene, then the liquids from the manure will be saved instead of escaping into the soil. An alternative would be to stack the dung somewhere you intend to plant something which will need a richly manured soil.

If it is impossible to obtain farmyard manures there are several processed types or organic substitutes. Cheaper than the bought manures, and

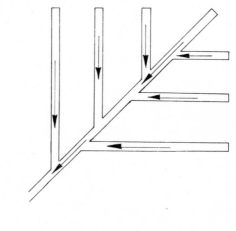

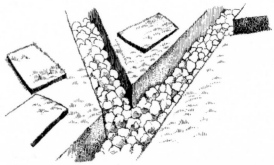

The best drainage systems are those laid in a herringbone pattern with the side drains running into the main drain. For a clinker system on a lawn neatly remove the turves, dig trenches 1½ to 2 feet deep, then fill to a depth of 12 inches with rubble before returning the topsoil and the turves. The main drain should run into a soakaway almost as good as animal manure, is garden compost. Details on how to make this are given on pages 62–63.

Not every gardener begins from scratch and many gardens needing manure have established plants around which it would be harmful to dig. In such cases the manure can be used as a mulch.

Mulching means covering the soil with a layer of organic material. Mulches keep the moisture in the soil down near the roots of the plant. Also, as the mulch disintegrates or becomes dragged into the soil by worms or forked in by ourselves, it enriches the soil and renders it more open and friable. Happily, by using a mulch to retain moisture, we also keep down weeds because the blanket we have spread over the soil does not allow light to reach seedling weeds and so they die.

One of the best and least expensive mulches is grass clippings from the lawn, but don't use these if the lawn has been recently treated with a weed-killer. Another good mulch, which, although it does not suppress them, makes the removal of weeds easier, is moist sedge peat. You can buy this anywhere. I mix it with a well-balanced organic fertiliser, in the proportion of a barrow-load of peat to a five-inch pot of fertiliser, and spread this mixture over the surface of the beds as a combined mulch and feed. If you have very poor soil, I recommend you to use peat this way and then to cover it with a layer of lawn clippings which will keep the peat moist and prevent it from drifting away.

Think of your soil as a store cupboard or a bank balance that must be replenished at intervals. Well-balanced artificial fertilisers are excellent but used alone they are not good enough. After a while they will no longer work because the soil will have become so starved of humus that the bacteria which teem in the soil and live on the humus can no longer change the chemicals into easily absorbed plant food. Remember, too, that the more the soil is cultivated the better it will be.

If you move to a new house, you may have to dig the garden whatever the time of year, but where you have the choice before planting, and particularly where soil is cleared as for vegetables or for bedding plants, begin in late autumn. Dig as deeply and as thoroughly as you have time or energy for. Make every possible use of the weather, a wonderful ally. Winter digging, for example, is especially valuable because it allows you to throw up the earth in great clods and leave them there. The winter frosts, rain, snow and wind will break them up much better than you will be able to yourself. The soil will become aerated, cleaned of insect pests, improved in texture

Simple digging to the depth of a spade is best carried out in winter especially on heavy clay soils when the weather can work on the clods to break them down to a plantable tilth

and condition so that when the time comes for planting or seed sowing, all that you will need to do is tap it with a fork or rake for it to crumble and make a fine tilth (a deep top layer of small particles through which it will be easy to draw a hoe or plunge a trowel).

In summer, any lumps larger than an egg should be broken down with the digging fork as work proceeds otherwise the soil will bake and become hard and be difficult to render down to a fine tilth. A good crumbly surface to soil makes a dust mulch which prevents too rapid evaporation of essential water from the soil.

When you dig, keep a bucket or an old basket near you to put all perennial weeds in as you see them, and afterwards destroy them. It is a good idea to lay them out somewhere to dry, then you will be able to burn them quickly. Never compost taprooted or creeping weeds (these include dandelion, dock, couch, convolvulus, thistle, nettles) if even small sections of root remain.

Garden lime is generally calcium hydroxide, or slaked lime. Ground chalk or limestone are the same thing in effect but slightly coarser in texture and therefore slower acting.

Calcium is an essential plant food, but most soils contain sufficient and lime for the garden is generally used to alter the alkalinity of the soil. But in addition it has other purposes. It helps to break up clay soils and it acts on the growth of soil fungi, encouraging some and discouraging others. Brassicas, for example, suffer from club root in an acid soil and lime discourages this fungus from attacking the roots of all members of the cabbage family. On the other hand potato scab flourishes in an alkaline soil, so we normally add lime where we plant brassicas and withhold it where we plant potatoes.

Lime is easy to apply. Just spread it on the top of the soil, preferably in autumn or early winter, and let the rains and frosts take it down. Naturally, it will not be used on a soil with a pH of 7·0 (neutral) or more for this soil is already alkaline. For acid soils apply slaked lime at the following rates: pH 6·0 from 6 ounces to 12 ounces per square yard, the lower figure for light and sandy soils and the higher for clay; pH 5·0 from 9 to 18 ounces per square yard and pH 4·0 from 12 to 24 ounces. These are, of course, guide figures or averages only and a little experimentation may prove helpful. Incidentally, all bonfire ash is good fertiliser and should be spread on the soil as soon as it cools.

If your soil is too acid or if it is really heavy after you have dug it, spread a handful of lime on each square yard of soil and allow the rain to wash it in. Do not try to save time by applying lime and animal manure at the same time for these two cancel each other's efforts. Allow at least six weeks after manuring the soil before adding lime.

Aim to have the top 9 or 12 inches of soil rich and fine and you will find that seedlings grow quickly and plants soon become established. If the soil below is broken up and well fed so much the better, particularly if it is a light soil. Never bring the subsoil to the surface. Unfortunately, this is what often happens on building sites robbed of topsoil.

In heavy soils and as an initial step in new gardens, soil may be double dug. This means removing the top spit (the depth of a spade's blade) a trench at a time, then forking over the subsoil, incorporating aerating manures at the same time and finally replacing the topsoil. It is easiest to do this by removing the top spit of the first row, wheeling it to the end of the plot to be dug and then, after forking the subsoil of the first row, throwing the topsoil of the second row over it. This operation is made much easier if you work with a string line to keep the rows straight. Double digging is recommended for all very heavy soils and particularly when a lawn is to be made on such soils. It is hard work!

The annual weeds are no great problem. They can be hoed, smothered with mulches or sprayed with chemicals. Weeds which break off along the roots, whose roots wander, or which send out runners, are the most difficult to eradicate.

Annual weeds can be dug into the soil – roots and all – and buried so that they rot, the perennials must be entirely removed. Never plant herbaceous plants, shrubs or trees in soil infected by weeds or their eradication will almost be impossible. Instead, dig and clean, then wait for weeds to reappear; fork and clean again, in bad cases, wait and clean again, before planting.

Many readers ask for a chemical which will solve their weeding problems for them. Unfortunately, a chemical cannot distinguish between plants you want to grow and those you want to keep out. So weedkillers should not be used indiscriminately. There are some that can be used on lawns where they will kill the weeds but not the grass. These are known as selective or hormone weedkillers. There are others that will kill every kind of plant. Yet more that will kill very young or emergent weed seedlings. More details are given on page 62.

Treat weeds with respect, not fear. Some can work for you. Pull up or hoe all annual weeds before they flower. If they are very tiny, they can be left after hoeing on the surface of the soil to shrivel. Otherwise, and especially if the weather is wet, rake them up and stack them on the compost heap.

Nettles, although perennials, will disappear completely if you just keep cutting them down. Compost the green tops but burn any roots.

Certainly, clay soils are heavy and back-breaking to work but they are really rich. Once they have become friable and comparatively easy to cultivate they are most rewarding. On the other hand, light, sandy soils, so easy to work, are usually poor and so we must do our utmost to make them a little heavier and not quite so easy to work. Gardeners with a plot that has been cultivated for years, town gardens are an example, may find that they have a dark-coloured, easy-to-work soil but which does not give very good results. In this case, the soil has become starved and will benefit by good loads of country manure or compost, seaweed-based composts or an organic fertiliser.

Making gardening easy

Routine is possibly the shortest cut to leisure. Certain regular jobs meticulously carried out enable you to keep up appearances in the garden and so give you a sense of achievement. Once the garden is made and designed, even if it is not fully planted, aim to keep it looking well, just as you try to keep the house tidy. It really should be no more trouble than that – cleaning and tidying, but in a different environment and with different tools. Never make more in the garden than you can look after. As I describe in another section, my own first borders were few and narrow. This meant that I could plant, weed and groom them in the time at my disposal. As they filled out and needed less attention I widened them and made others. Gradually the whole of the garden has come under our control.

Be sure to invest in good tools and efficient machines. It is worth skimping on plants to get these first.

Routine means watching the months. While one can beat the calendar, there are certain jobs which it pays one to do as soon as the time is ripe or the weather suitable, this applies particularly to pruning.

Owners of lawns will find that much of their routine is determined by the grass. Use the first opportunity of a dry weekend in spring to get the grass mown. These mowings can be used for the first mulch to suppress weeds which will already be germinating in the borders. Place the mowings right over and smother annual weeds that may even already be flowering.

Immediately after mowing, trim the edge with long-handled edging shears and remove any weeds near the edge. I pull a large polythene bag along with me to collect the debris.

To save time when you mow the lawn, place two or more of these bags, according to the size of your lawn, at intervals and push the mowings in these as you come to them. This will save you walking too far to deposit them in one place. You will be able to do this later. The bags are quite easy to pull along when necessary. Alternatively, two or more polythene or hessian sheets can be placed on the grass, according to area, and these can act as the dumping ground to save possibly lengthy walks at each emptying of the grass box.

Personally, I cannot bear to see edgings too strictly defined and I would rather walk along the garden before mowing pushing a few cascading plants back, securing them with a bamboo and then restoring them to their original positions than have a cut edge and an area of bare soil next to the grass. But this is a matter of personal taste and something gardeners must decide for themselves.

It is possible to use manufactured lawn edging like lengths of corrugated aluminium to cut down work. This also can be used to define an area round trees growing in grass, paving or some other ground cover. Bricks or paving edgings of all kinds may also be used but they should be set low enough for the mower to pass over them.

Lengths of specially manufactured corrugated aluminium will help to keep lawn edges neat. They should fit tightly against the lawn edge and be pressed firmly into the surrounds

Plan your garden so that it is easy to run. Keep lawns simple, avoid curves that are difficult to negotiate with the mower, hard-to-get-at corners, and trees and shrubs that hang so low that it is difficult to mow under them. Keep lawns on level ground. A lawn on a steep slope is difficult and can be dangerous to mow without the right equipment.

Place trees and shrubs inside borders rather than isolate them. This will avoid hand clipping round their bases.

Arrange your borders so that plants that can stand unintentional clipping by the mower are nearest the edges; thymes and ericas are examples.

Choose perennials that need little division and no staking rather than those which demand a great deal of attention.

Plan borders that are mixed so that you do not have to lift and clear plants twice a year to fit in with bedding schemes.

Place stepping stones among plants in wide borders so that you can reach plants easily.

When you plan a hedge with a border in front of it, also allow room for a service path between the two, large enough to take yourself comfortably while working plus a machine or a barrow to help you when trimming the hedge.

On page 7, I have explained how mulching with organic substances can make less work as well as enriching the soil. Decorative mulches of pebbles, shingle or gravel can be used round trees or groups of plants to intensify the effect of contrast of textures and shapes. These mulches keep the soil cool and help to keep the weeds down.

Pebble mulches are especially decorative when used around the moisture-loving perennials with which they associate so well. They also help in preserving the conditions which these plants enjoy – a cool, moist soil

Where a very weedy patch exists and plant roots might become too disturbed in one's efforts to remove the weeds, these can be killed by laying black polythene over them and weighting it down. Even strong brown paper will have this effect. It needs to be left in position for a few months where the weeds are very bad. I have successfully cleared dandelions, docks and convolvulus this way.

For the smaller garden the basic hand tools are sufficient; indeed, sometimes they are better. But make sure that they are always kept in good condi-

tion and buy the best available. It is not an easy discipline to follow, but it is worthwhile cleaning tools and giving them a quick rub over with an oily rag at the end of each working session in the garden.

It is well worthwhile, too, having a special place in the garage or shed for each of your tools so you know exactly where it is each time it is required for any particular task.

It's far better to buy a few basic tools of top quality than to spend the same sum on a wider range of dubious quality, for breakages at an inconvenient time can be frustrating indeed.

The basic tools, without which gardening simply cannot be carried out are a spade, a fork, a rake, secateurs and shears. As you use them you will gradually find that another tool would simplify one task or be more convenient for others and so you will enlarge your armoury. A hand fork and trowel, a hoe of some kind and perhaps a scarifier or cultivator may very well prove to be required.

Eventually, when you are a veteran gardener you will find that you keep specialised tools for certain tasks and that your range is very wide indeed. But learn from personal experience and convenience rather than impersonal advice.

Try to tailor your garden tools to your own height and strength. A border fork is smaller and lighter than a digging fork and if you are small and not too strong you can get more work done with the smaller model than the larger. With handle lengths for tools such as rakes and hoes, the most convenient and easily managed height or length is one which is some 6 to 9 inches less than your own height. Longer than this the handle will get in your way, shorter you will find you are having to lean forward and so tire yourself.

Many tools can be bought specially or adapted for left-handed gardeners and more and more tools are being made for elderly or partially disabled gardeners. A hand fork mounted on a long handle, for example, enables those who cannot bend too well to weed and fork over a wide border which would otherwise entail kneeling, bending and even crawling among the plants. And for those who can kneel but find it difficult both to get down to this position and then to rise again, there are special kneeling stools with tall handles.

New materials have been very helpful to the gardener. Stainless steel and chrome-treated rust-resistant metals slide through sticky soils with less effort and are so much easier to clean. Aluminium alloy handles are lighter in weight and stronger. Plastic-coated handles are smooth, cannot splinter and again are easily cleaned. Plastic buckets, garden trugs, watering-cans and even wheelbarrows are so much lighter in weight, are easily cleaned and cannot rust.

Electricity is coming increasingly into the garden and a number of hand tools are conveniently powered with lightweight, rechargeable batteries.

Finally, two products which may not be regarded strictly as tools but which I find invaluable when working in the garden: gloves and labels. Garden gloves can be light cotton, light or heavy plastic or even heavy leather. I compromise and use a medium-weight plastic and I find that not only do my hands

stay cleaner, but they are protected from scratches, cuts and bruises. I always keep two pairs going, for they are apt to become moist and unpleasant inside.

With the possible exception of certain plants, such as trees, which may be unmistakable, every plant in the garden should be accompanied by a label. It is almost impossible to remember the name of everything and at certain times of the year impossible to be quite sure of the location of some plants. There are many types of label and it pays to get the best you can afford, for one which is torn to tatters in winter winds or which quickly becomes illegible is simply a waste of time.

Plan for convenience

Just as a well-planned kitchen saves one a great deal of unnecessary work, so can a well-planned garden. If you are making a new garden you have every opportunity to plan your plot so that it affords you more time for leisure and pottering than it takes to do the heavier work. And even if yours is an established garden, it is necessary to look at it critically every once in a while to ask yourself if one boring task could not be eliminated or one time-consuming job made shorter.

Although so many modern methods have been welcomed inside the house, much needs improving in the garden itself. Quite often just a few changes in the plan could make a world of difference. Ask yourself what job takes longest, and what you like doing least and see if you can re-arrange your garden from these two points.

The size of the plot and the shape and height of the house must be taken into account. In your mind's eye treat the garden as a room. Make it of pleasing proportions. Push the walls back as far as you can, even if this is only illusory. For intimacy, make a ceiling, remember that quite literally, the sky is the limit. A spreading tree, a row of cordons trained over the patio, a vine running along the beams or rails overhead will give a delightful feeling of privacy in a crowded locality or in a tiny garden.

Furnish the walls and set furniture about. In the home, furniture does not normally dwarf the walls and in the same way a bungalow does not look

well cowering under a tall tree nor does a tall house look well with a tiny skirt of shrubs. If these features do exist, then plan to bring them into harmony. The area around the house and the plants and other features it holds need to be planned in relation to the house. Certainly group plants together, but do not get a forest in one spot with a bare alpine scree next to it. Remember your home; you do not pile all the furniture in one place but you site it carefully, playing one piece against the other.

Arranged like this, a garden can be the real hub of a home. There can be a games area, maybe a miniature putting green – easily made! One wall can be used for a dartboard, an archer's bull's-eye and perhaps one of the static tennis games to provide both practice and recreation. A swimming pool is no longer an impossible dream. Good sized prefabricated pools can be bought and may be placed on paving or sunk into the ground.

In such gardens paving plays a great part. But I must try to dissuade any anti-gardeners who feel that it would be really labour-saving only if the whole area was concreted and have done with it! There is no reason why the whole area should not be paved, but one ought to plan paving and paving patterns and their relationship to plants just as much as any other part of the garden. Concrete, not very attractive on its own, can be hidden by coloured tiles, given new textures by using pebbles and other surfaces. Sprawling shrubs and other

A children's play area on a patio

plants may be used as furnishing to break up arid expanses and to throw pretty and well-shaped shadows.

If seeking for a labour-saving theme, and the contemporary gardens are too radical, too extreme, too austere for you, consider making a wild garden from your plot. Here, two essentials are most important. One must make a really careful choice of materials, suitable plants to be set at apparent random or in a haphazard pattern of planting. Plants should consist entirely of trees and shrubs of an informal nature: silver birch rather than magnolia, untrained pyracantha, cotoneaster, mountain ash and other semi-wild trees with perhaps blossoming kinds for spring. These should be underplanted with dwarf shrubs such as azaleas and with little glades of ground cover plants, bulb flowers and tiny cyclamen (see the section on ground cover plants). The path should meander, never cut through the rather dense woodland. It could be made of stepping stones, unevenly shaped slabs or circular concrete blocks.

Sometimes changes in garden design have to be made for reasons of pure utility. A family with young children may move into a house with an entirely unsuitable garden, or an elderly couple

may require something more labour-saving. In planning these 'purposeful' gardens, one should first determine the essentials, then once the features are chosen they may be fitted into the overall scheme.

For young children there should be play features such as a sandpit, paddling pool, climbing frame, swing or Wendy house and, where possible, these should be grouped in a suitable area so that lawns are not battered by the thunder of tiny feet or herbaceous borders smashed and broken by flying balls. Children in the family must certainly be catered for. They should feel that the garden belongs to them and is not merely a show place into which they are not allowed to trespass. On the other hand, they must learn to respect the plants you buy and tend.

Places most liked by children are the hidden areas – or supposedly hidden – where they can play 'hide' games: the land that runs beside the hedge, the glen behind the border made shady and hidden from grown-up eyes, the areas under and behind trees, even the stout limbs of large trees. Play areas of mystery can be made so simply, merely by making a footway that enables one to walk (or run) round the whole perimeter of the garden. If the path winds, is hidden, turns occasionally into stepping stones or leads through a gate or over a tiny but safe bridge, so much the better.

A little piece of rising land can seem very high indeed to a small child. A flight of steps to the top where he can look out is ideal, and provides a definite right of way so that the rest of the hill does not become trodden down. I did this on my own peat hill for my son when he was small. Now I find the steps extremely useful for weeding and otherwise tending my plants.

A large tree can have a lookout platform built a few feet from the ground – it does not have to be high. A safe flight of steps needs to lead up to it. This should have at least one firm hand rail. The platform could serve a double purpose. Hooks fastened to the edges could be used to assemble a 'tent' from an old sheet, the platform becoming the roof.

Wendy houses can be merged attractively into the garden and can be made even more realistic if they have their own little hedge or screen. Avoid thorny shrubs like roses, though you can plant the lovely thornless rose Zéphirine Drouhin, perfect for such a hedge and with beautiful blooms. Avoid berried shrubs in case the children are tempted to use them for 'cooking' and never plant a laburnum tree in the children's area, for the little pea-like pods of seeds are very poisonous indeed.

A play place for very small children or toddlers needs to be in sight of the house. If a sandpit is to be made it should be protected in some way from the prevailing wind to prevent the sand being blown about too much. Not often seen in gardens, but in use at the end of many country drives which lead on to a busy road, is a large mirror. By using this you could tuck the play area out of the way of the main garden yet clearly visible in the mirror from the kitchen window.

Wigwams and tents are not so pretty in small gardens and tend to become blown down on windy days, but you can plan an Indian tepee by using climbing plants and some strong posts. A permanent climbing plant like clematis or polygonum will cover the posts all the year round, but temporary effects can be obtained by using runner beans or gourds for the summer months only.

Give the children a scribbling wall on the patio where they will play quite absorbed for hours. No need to paint this black – a matt green will do just as well. When they have passed the scribbling stage, targets for archery can be painted or hung on it.

Water is an essential in child's play. A rain barrel neatly painted to suit the house will prove useful in many ways. A tap in the garden means that you will be left in peace in the house and water games played outdoors! You will also have a good source of soft water for your house plants and flower arrangements. Place the barrel beneath a rainwater pipe and be sure to include the overflow pipe. The best way to do this is to make a hole in the centre of the floor of the barrel. In this fix tightly a length of galvanised iron tubing which comes just below the top of the barrel. This will mean not only that the barrel does not overflow in time of heavy rain, but that any insects, larvae or debris floating on the top are sucked down into the drain below. This is impossible in a plastic rain barrel, so arrange its base so that it leans very slightly in the direction where it will be safest for an overspill to flow.

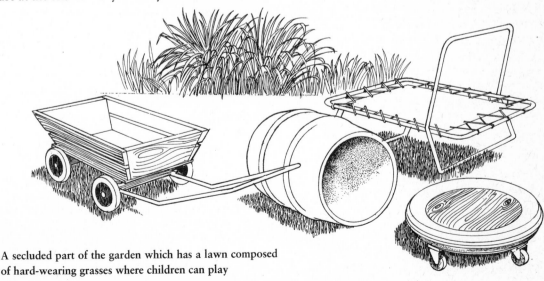

A secluded part of the garden which has a lawn composed of hard-wearing grasses where children can play

Furniture that grows

How you place and group your trees, their shape and shadows, their relation to your house and to their surroundings, determines not only the design of your garden but also its character and, indeed, your own personality. So make sure that the furniture is in the right place. Plan the sites for your trees and shrubs first of all. Indeed, if you are looking for a completely labour-saving garden you can fill it with these plants alone. But for those who, like me, enjoy the mixtures and associations of plants, aim to get all the permanent features established so that you can create at leisure the foreground interest and complete your scheme with flowers and other plants.

Your garden may be much improved by a background of trees. These need not be large, dense and green, when they are liable to shut out the light, but should be chosen to suit the very place you have for them. You may, for example, like a flowering cherry but feel that there is no room for the spreading boughs. In this case, you can buy an upright form, in shape like a Lombardy poplar.

Slow-growing plants suit a small garden best. Among these are maples, some conifers including the umbrella pines, the dwarf hybrid Kurume azaleas and the lovely liquidambar.

For autumn colour, grow the snowy mespilus or amelanchier which blossoms in spring and forms a neat little tree. Also small species of berberis, and *Cotinus coggygria*, the smoke bush.

When you plant to make a screen, avoid heavy evergreens or you will give a gloomy atmosphere to the place to be screened! A mixture of evergreen and deciduous shrubs or trees is effective. In small gardens, plants with feathery leaves or a light dainty habit look best. *Tamarix pentandra* is really beautiful and can be kept from reaching its natural 12 feet by pruning; colutea or bladder senna is among the easiest of all shrubs to grow and will thrive on poor stony soil; cotoneasters are evergreen, berry-bearing but dainty and very varied; *Fuchsia magellanica riccartonii* and the more arching *F. m. gracilis* are the hardy little red and purple fuchsias you see so much as hedges in the West Country; hippophae or sea buckthorn is a good tree for seaside districts to screen a garden against the wind.

If you have a small garden never plant a tree without knowing something of its rate of growth or in later years you may regret your earlier impetuosity. But if you do desperately want a tree which might grow too large, a weeping willow for example, make up your mind to have it removed when it reaches the size you want and replace it with a young one. This is much better than lopping and mutilating the one you have when it becomes oversized.

So many people write to ask me the names of trees and shrubs that will grow quickly and so make a new garden look well established. But unfortunately those plants that grow very quickly are often too gross for the average garden. Not only do they grow fast but they go on growing – roots as well as tops! So choose plants that take their time and need not be uprooted in years to come. Remember that for every foot of tree above the ground there are several exploring feet of root underground.

The growth rate of trees and shrubs is determined partly by the type of plant, partly by the soil in which it is planted, partly by the weather and partly by the care which it receives. It is impossible to lay down any hard and fast rules. Generally speaking, however, when a tree or shrub is first planted it takes at least a year to establish itself and grow a new root system. In the second year it consolidates itself and in the third year noticeable growth appears. After the third year, progress is more rapid according to the time it takes for the tree or shrub to reach maturity. Some mature early, others take many years.

We should not be too conservative in our use of trees and shrubs. On the Continent fruit – apples, pears, cherries and grapes – are trained to make arbours, or covered ways round a house. Decorative trees, cherries and crabs for example, could be used the same way if fruit was not needed.

Many shrubs can be used as informal hedges, provided you have the space for about an ultimate four-foot spread. They really are little work and I go into much more detail later on.

Shrubs are bushes, and indeed are bushy for they do not grow in such a way that the branches spring from a main trunk. Like most things, the division is not really clear cut and many plants listed as shrubs are really, or will become, small trees.

As we shall see, some perennial herbaceous plants demand a certain amount of attention every few years but there are trees and shrubs which will give you as much colour and which need no attention at all and which, bare or evergreen, will grace your garden all year. They come in all shapes, sizes and colours and vary from real miniatures, low, ground-hugging spreading types (prostrate) some of which will fall prettily over a rock or the top of a wall, to those that tower gracefully to the sky in lovely columnar shapes. The true miniatures are also suitable for sinks, rock gardens and small gardens.

The height of the trunk of a tree varies according to its type. With fastigiate trees, of which the Lombardy poplar is perhaps the best known, the trunk is mostly hidden by branches which reach upwards and roughly follow its line. A standard tree, on the other hand, has the maximum length of trunk and usually a wide top. Such a tree will need strong staking for it will not bend to the wind like the first, and it might snap.

For small gardens, a half standard is often best for not only does it not dominate the scene but it is easier to care for. Fruit trees that are half standards are easier to spray and the fruit is easier to pick. For the same reason many people prefer a bush-type tree which has a very short trunk. Not all trees can be thus classified, for many grow in their own natural manner, but much depends on the means of propagation employed by the nurseryman. Where parts of an ornamental tree benefit by being grafted on a stronger growing stock this is usually done. A good catalogue will contain this information.

Some trees have lovely pendulous branches and are known as weeping trees. These are delightful as specimen trees to grace a lawn or to be used to block out an unattractive view. Many are far too large for the average small garden. Ash, for example, will grow so large that one can sit below its branches as though in a room, but there are daintier weeping trees, not so well known, such as the silver leaved pear, *Pyrus salicifolia pendula*.

Evergreens are never in fact just that! Their colour range is great and includes golds, blues, oranges, light and dark greens, soft downy greys, variegations of many kinds including stripes and slashes and spotted foliage.

There is an impression that trees and shrubs are best spaced out to avoid overcrowding. The natural growth in woods and forests belies this impression and although it is true that in their later and fully mature stages these plants may suffer through overcrowding, it is probably fair to say that in the seedling stage and, in many cases, in the first ten years or so of their lives, they will benefit rather than suffer through close proximity of friendly neighbours. They will give shade and shelter to each other, help keep the ground clear at their feet, and present a more concentrated and powerful picture. So if you want to get a permanent look about your garden in a hurry, there is no reason why you should not plant thicker than recommended and thin out later, when the plants begin to jostle each other. If, when you plant with this in mind, you line all the planting holes with sphagnum peat, you will find, when the time comes for transplanting, that the plants have developed a good fibrous root system and are comparatively easy to lift. You will also find that the transplanted shrubs or trees grown this way are more likely to survive a move and to recover quickly after transplanting than if you had allowed them to develop a strong taproot or more thong-like roots which they would do more strongly without peat.

If trees and shrubs are not present the garden loses moisture, for roots search deep in times of drought and leaves constantly produce a humid microclimate suitable for the growth of other plants. Equally important, trees and shrubs are labour-saving, requiring little attention after their initial planting.

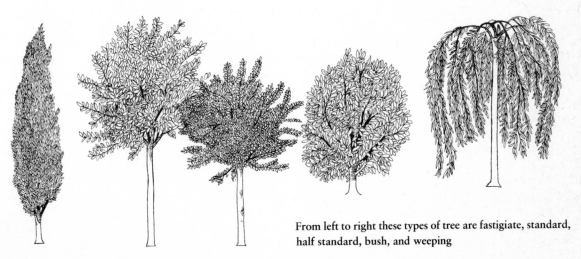

From left to right these types of tree are fastigiate, standard, half standard, bush, and weeping

15

Planting and pruning

There are two kinds of trees and shrubs; deciduous (those that shed their leaves in the autumn), and evergreens (which keep their leaves and constantly renew them). Those in the first group may be planted at any time when the branches are bare, usually from early November until the middle of March (though November and March are the best times). If the season is late, sometimes planting may go on until a later date.

There is one important exception, the deciduous magnolias (others are evergreen) which should be planted in spring, April or May. Most evergreens do best when planted after the shortest day rather than late autumn.

It is possible, indeed preferable, to prepare the sites for shrubs and trees before they are received from the nursery. The holes should be dug leaving plenty of room for the roots to be spread, and a good portion of decayed animal manure, leafmould, peat or garden compost and a handful of bonemeal incorporated with the soil which is to go back under and around the young plants' roots.

The methods of planting trees and shrubs are the same, except that in most cases a tree must be provided with a firm stake in its early years. The stake should run vertically quite near the trunk and be at least a foot deep in the ground and a little higher than the trunk and one should be secured to the other. To do this in my own garden I have used everything from scrim, linen, wire buffered by sheets of rubber tyre and the specially made tree tie, rather like a dog collar. The latter is by far and away the most efficient and well worth the few pence one pays for it.

Quite the most important thing is firm planting. This means noting the different layers of roots, spreading them out naturally, and packing soil between them as well as over them. If you dig the hole a little larger than you really need, you will have room to work well; it is important to fork over the base to allow roots quickly to penetrate. You will see on the base of the trunk or stem the old soil mark indicating the depth at which the plant originally grew. You must see that after planting this mark is at the same soil level as it was before. There are exceptions to this rule: heathers, lavenders, thymes and similar bunchy shrubs should be planted deeper.

A great deal will depend upon the condition of the plant when it reaches you. If you have bought container-grown plants, which, incidentally, may be planted at any time of the year, water both the plant and the site well the day before planting. Then just remove the container, disturbing the root ball as little as possible, and insert it in the hole made ready for it. Fill the hole, cover the top of the container soil with a little new soil and press down with the heel of the foot. Test by pulling the plant a little to one side. It should really be immovable.

Many trees and shrubs arrive from the nursery with the root ball securely bound in sacking. This should be soaked by immersion in a bucket. When the bubbles cease to rise, remove the plant, allow to drain, and uncover and plant, disturbing the root ball as little as possible. Other plants, such as roses, have roots with no soil on them at all.

In a dry season, I think that it is well worthwhile standing shrubs, trees, and especially roses, with

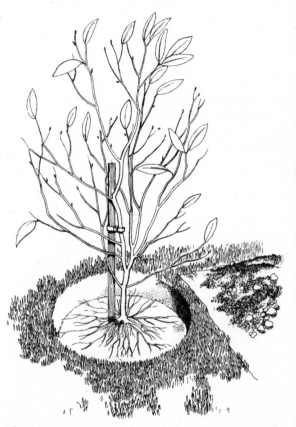

After planting a specimen shrub in a lawn in a well-worked, nutritious soil to the correct depth and staking firmly, neaten the hole to a uniform shape, usually either a square or a circle

16

their roots in water for an hour or two while you are preparing the soil for them. I always place well-soaked peat immediately round the roots of plants. Usually the day before planting I have a barrow or bucket ready filled with peat and with water added. Peat takes a long time to absorb the water and after twenty-four hours it is nicely moist and ready for use.

Often plants arrive at a time when the soil is unsuitable for planting – it may be frozen or sodden. In this case plants should be heeled in until the conditions are more favourable. At times I have had to keep mine heeled in for months. They seem to come to no harm but I find that the soft paper labels attached by some nurserymen tend to become weather-beaten and indecipherable. It is wise, therefore, to write new labels. To heel in, open a trench in some site away from strong winds. Lay the roots in the trench with the tops of the plants slanting at about 45 degrees. Cover the roots with peat and then throw soil over this. Firm it down.

Heel in shrubs which arrive when the soil is frozen or sodden in a sheltered part of the garden so that they are firmly anchored at an angle of 45 degrees

Frosts after planting affect the roothold of shrubs and trees. They become loosened, and when blown about a hole forms in the soil round the base of the stem or trunk. If this is left water will enter and may rot the roots, so go round the garden after gales and tread the plants in firmly. Do not do this while the soil is still sticky from frost but wait until it becomes drier.

Drought at any time of year is damaging to newly planted trees and shrubs. Evergreens in particular suffer. Not many of these can stand cold east and north winds which can be very drying, especially to foliage. Mulching round the roots in March helps to keep the roots moist. If the soil is already very dry it is wise to water the roots before applying the mulch. Hay and chopped bracken are often used for this purpose. I have seen polythene used effectively but this must be weighted down. During spring droughts and on until early summer it is wise to spray the foliage with clean water.

Gardeners, who like me have had to clear a little land at a time, may want to plant into grassed areas before the final borders are cut out or the garden finally landscaped. This is quite all right so long as a good area of soil is kept free round the base of the plant. You need a circle 4 feet in diameter for trees for the first four years at least. Later, if you wish, grass can be allowed to grow right up near the base. Mulching will keep this clear and cool at the same time. A smaller circle, some 2 feet, will do for shrubs. I give more details in the chapter on new gardens.

Pruning appears to bedevil many amateur gardeners and I find, as a general rule, that men are inclined to overprune often with no knowledge and little skill, while women do not prune enough! My advice is if you are not sure let it stay as it is and do no more than clean up by removing dead flower heads and obviously sickly or very weak stems.

Newly planted flowering shrubs are helped to grow to a good shape by pruning in their early years. After they have obviously settled down, in the second or third year after planting, look each one over and take away the tops of the strongest-growing branches. Cut off about 6 inches. After this let them grow unaided and they should then make a good shape. Invariably, a good catalogue will advise you on pruning procedure for the plants you buy but here are a few general rules.

Shrubs flower either on stems (usually referred to as wood) made during the previous year or they flower on the current year's growth: Usually, the spring-flowering types bear bloom on the previous year's wood. Pruning should be carried out immediately flowering is over, and its purpose should be to encourage new growth. I would like to point out that gardeners who grow spring shrubs for cutting actually prune as they gather. When doing this, it is wise to look round the bushes and to take out twisted, weak and crossing stems and also those which are growing too close to the soil where this is not desired.

Summer- and autumn-flowering shrubs which flower on the current year's growth should be pruned in March. In this case, cut away the wood made the previous year to the lowest bud. This will promote new, vigorous growth. Always cut a stem near a bud but not so close that you injure the growing tissue. Snags and long pieces of bare stem should be avoided for disease often affects these and can spread over an entire plant.

Owners of small gardens often like to keep plants pruned to keep them within bounds and under control. Where it is necessary to cut a shrub or tree, never lop branches halfway, leaving a mutilated plant. After pruning, a plant ought still to look lovely and not violated. It is better to take a complete bough right away down close to the main stem

of the shrub or tree and to do this every few years treating a different part of the plant than to hack at it annually. This is a good method to use for plants grown for their arching beauty and which have got out of hand.

Where you want to allow trees to remain but fear that they will cast too much shade, you can safely remove lower branches to let in light. Again, this should be done by cutting them flush with the trunk.

Variegated plants sometimes produce a shoot of green – their original colour. This should be cut out, or the whole plant may revert.

Always use good sharp secateurs and efficient saws and pruners.

Making the boundary

Too much screening can make your garden dark, small and uneasily confined. So do not rush to fence yourself in. Just as a lace or net curtain will effectively veil a room from street eyes, so will a comparatively skimpy curtain of foliage. To begin with, it's an idea to plant, for example, a row of runner beans, sweet peas, golden rod or sunflowers, as a 'token' fence until you see – literally, perhaps – which way the wind blows.

We usually find that some sort of garden boundary has been installed, to define our property. For economic reasons, this is usually a wire and post fence and it is generally unattractive.

One of the best means of making use of the basic post and wire boundary fence is to grow on it some vigorous material which will quickly form some sort of screen. One of the best of these is the awkwardly named *Polygonum baldschuanicum,* or Russian vine. This is a rampant grower which can make as much as 20 feet of growth in a single season. It gives a foam of creamy pink flowers in summer but alas it is deciduous and loses its leaves in the winter.

Some climbing and rambler roses will make a good and quick-growing screen which, again, can be trained along existing wires. Annuals, such as tall nasturtiums, make a fine summer screen. I have seen espalier fruit trees trained along the wires which were set about a foot above each other.

The first thing to do is to ask oneself why a screen

or fence is necessary. The most important aspect of a screen or fence is to protect the garden against wind. A few washing days will show you from which way the prevailing wind blows. Cast an eye over any large trees growing nearby. If their outlines show signs of the sloping growth caused by strong sweeping winds, be prepared! You will certainly need some kind of wind break to cut down their damaging power. Whether this is a dense one such as a fence, or an open one such as a row of plants, is up to you to decide. There are many decorative trees and shrubs which will grow happily in such a situation.

If you need to shut out an ugly view or make a screen in just one spot, you need a spreading tree or large shrub – not necessarily an evergreen for even bare branches make good covers. Most small flowering trees are safest near the house since their roots do not penetrate far. Fast growers like weeping willows, poplar or metasequoia have large ever-searching roots, which might upset the foundations of your house.

A grouping of mature trees provides both a windscreen and boundary in this very pretty garden. The colourful island bed with its mixed planting of perennials and annuals backed by pink roses demonstrates just how successful such a feature can be. Good use, too, has been made of the house wall with the climbing roses planted so that the flowers of the two varieties intermingle

Many readers write to ask me for the names of fast-growing trees for screens and though I may be dampening their spirits I always tell them that any tree which grows very fast is also going to grow really big. The best permanent plant screens are those which take their time.

Where only complete screening will suffice, a timber fence is the quickest and cheapest answer. This can quickly and easily be disguised by growing plants. Many evergreens and others will grow up and along or can be trained to hug a new fence prettily and in time will hide it. A mixture of evergreen and deciduous plants will present a wide range of possibilities, depending upon soil and aspect.

The best wooden fences are oak, but they can also be bought in larch, pine, deal or cedar in heights varying from 3 to 7 feet. If they are untreated they will need to be painted with a preservative. Untreated wood rots quickly.

Split chestnut is a cheap, rustic form of fencing. Checker board is a 'woven' variation of a wooden fence. I should advise you to visit a garden shop or centre and see and compare various forms and prices.

Wattle hurdles, like those used by the farmer, are very cheap but not very long lasting. These are best used as a quick temporary fence which acts also as a windbreak behind newly planted shrubs and trees to protect them while they are young.

If you do not like the closed-in effect of a tall fence, use a low fence and erect a more open screen some little distance from it on which roses or some other plant can be trained. Make sure the screen is stout enough to stand the buffeting of the wind.

If you dislike the hard lines of a fence and would like to get an impression of a leafy hedge there are many plants such as evergreen, winter-flowering and variegated honeysuckles, ornamental vines including the Virginia creepers, clematis, and passion flowers which can be trained against the fence, but are not weighty enough to pull it out of shape. *Polygonum baldschuanicum* is very quick and rampant growing but may get out of hand unless its roots can be restricted. In the first year you can sow seed of annuals like canary creeper, morning glory or Blue Coco variety of climbing French beans to cover the fence temporarily.

Alternatively, you can erect a series of metal poles, rustic posts or trellis on which you can grow one of the lovely flowering screen plants, including 'pillar' roses.

A garden fence consisting merely of a few separated strands of wire can have fruit trees trained along it. Perhaps you can co-operate with your neighbour, and both plant trees alternately. This way you can be sure of having enough varieties to pollinate your trees successfully so that you have good crops of fruit.

Fibreglass has tremendous possibilities and is now being used in several colours to make good screens, roofs and other garden accessories. It is not affected by weather and is strong. A new 'clean' look and a new maintenance-free permanence is provided with plastic fencing, mainly in ranch-type style.

Modern fabricated stone can be obtained in several shapes from which one can make most attractive semi-open walls. They make a pleasant boundary without the closed-in effect of a solid wall. These open-work walls are just the thing for a patio or a sun bay as well as for boundaries.

Walls can now be as varied as paths, in fact. For example, you can have a plain solid base against which you can grow flowering or fruiting plants under a pretty open-work top.

This is not the place, I feel, to go into a long description of wall-making techniques. But I would just suggest that it is sometimes forgotten that a good solid wall requires a good solid foundation if subsidence is not to cause trouble in the future.

We are so accustomed to seeing walls made of brick or stone that we tend to forget that there are now so many other materials which can be used. The advantage of most of them is that they are so easy to handle that even the unskilled worker can build a good wall. Artificial stone of all kinds, and concrete open-work blocks can be laid simply and effectively.

Manufacturers usually supply fences in do-it-yourself form, either in separate pieces or made up into large panels.

Although the association of plants and wall (and particularly in this case of shrubs and wall) can be very beautiful, this partnership is seldom exploited by the modern gardener.

The plants need not always be seen against a wall. They can cut across the wall line. There are times where a plant and a wall make a patterned barrier. Walls can be built and shaped in such a manner that where the wall dips, a plant rises. Here plants of a distinctive shape can be used.

Evergreens will become as dense a screen as the wall itself, while deciduous trees or shrubs will bring seasonal variety and colour changes, even in certain cases, blossom also.

Among the evergreens some of the junipers and

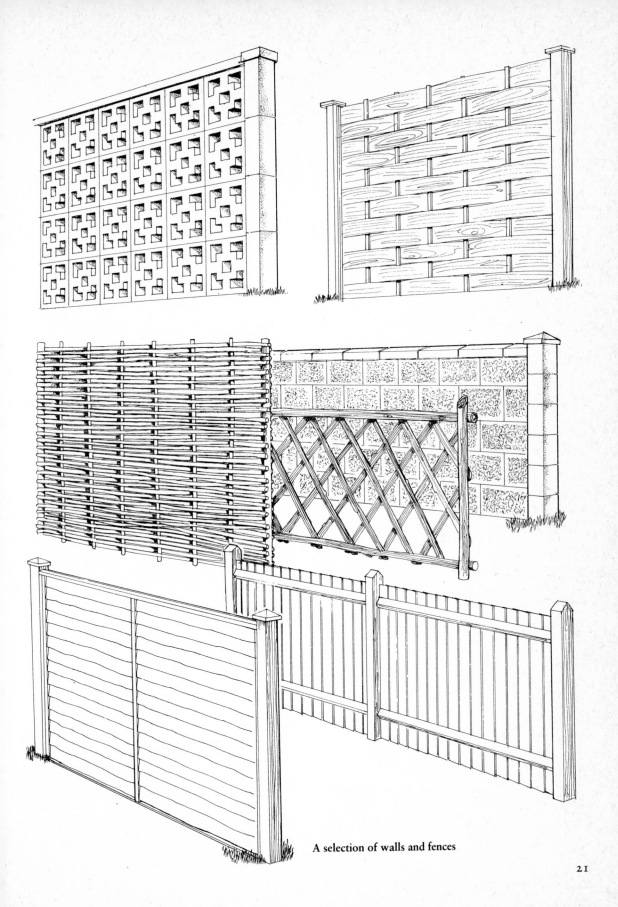

A selection of walls and fences

chamaecyparis are beautifully columnar, and there are others which will bring hues of blue-green and yellow to the scene. Larger growing are the upright or fastigiate deciduous trees such as birch, *Betula pendula fastigiata*; hornbeam, *Carpinus betulus columnaris* and *pyramidalis*; hawthorn, *Crataegus monogyna stricta*; beech, *Fagus sylvatica fastigiata*; poplar, *Populus nigra italica*; flowering cherry, *Prunus* Amanagowa (syn. *P. serrulata erecta*); oak, *Quercus robur fastigiata*; and *Robinia pseudoacacia fastigiata*, which may be too large for small gardens but which could be used as a wall-screen at the boundaries of a large garden where the harsh line of a straight wall would not be desirable.

Where areas of grass have been eliminated and in their place paving or other flooring materials have been laid down, the hedge can play a decorative role and may be so colourful that it acts as a permanent flower bed.

For example it can consist of three or more parts or layers: shall we say, a background of purple-leaved prunus, a lower hedge of yellow privet or chamaecyparis and an even lower hedge of santolina or lavender and perhaps even lower than this, covering the ground and forming a border, a strip of heather. There are other equally effective combinations of plants which can be used.

The type of soil is not a great problem here, because as I have already remarked, although most ericaceous plants need an acid or peaty soil, there are many varieties which are lime tolerant. Among these are the winter-flowering heathers which ensure a band of colour from October to April. After flowering the plants can be clipped to keep them neat and they will continue to give a band of green through the summer. Soil on the site of a hedge must be well prepared and any deficiencies remedied before planting.

Hedges

A hedge gives a thick permanent screen but you should decide what its purpose is to be before you plant it. If it is merely to set the boundary of your plot, then make it as unobtrusive as possible. If you want to turn your garden into an outdoor room as it were, then make good green walls from dense hedges, but cut attractive doors or windows into them also. Suitable plants for such a hedge would be beech and hawthorn, which can be clipped. Mixed or tapestry hedges can be very attractive, especially if an evergreen like holly is mixed with deciduous trees such as beech with its fresh soft green silky leaves in spring and the copper beech which brings a note of purple-bronze. Privet is really not good for a hedge because it robs the soil so badly and is very dull. Cotoneaster and lonicera (which needs constant clipping) are both evergreen and good for small gardens. Beech, green and copper mixed three to one, is pretty and keeps its autumn brown leaves on all winter. So does hornbeam which is useful for heavy clay soil. Snowberry or symphoricarpos gives a mass of berries but loses its leaves in winter. Hawthorn is probably the cheapest and most effective deciduous hedge. Holly is the best evergreen and,

like hawthorn, forms a dense barrier and keeps everything out. You can mix the two alternately. Box is compact but very slow growing and attracts snails. Thuya, a conifer, is evergreen or evergold.

Quite often a fence, low wall, even a low hedge, exists already round a garden but is not in itself important enough to give the privacy required. In this case plants grown as a screen are more important than closely grown and clipped hedge plants.

Most nurserymen stock a supply of hedging plants. These vary considerably in price but, as one might imagine, the common hedging such as privet, is very much cheaper than say, myrtle. Hedging plants vary in size but a good size is around $1\frac{1}{2}$ to 2 feet. This means that you have very young plants at an early stage in the life of your hedge and so can train it as you will.

Annuals are excellent plants for those gardeners who like to experiment for the results are quickly seen. This delightful and imaginative association of colour and texture is the result of sowing the annual grass *Lagurus ovatus* with *Tagetes patula* Suttons Goldie. Yellow African marigolds complete this lovely grouping

Generally speaking, you can keep hedges under control according to how you trim or clip them. The ultimate height of a tree or shrub given in a botanical or gardening book may be no guide for a hedge. With beech, for example, a specimen tree may grow as high as 80 feet. A hedge will tower to 15 feet or more but it may also be kept, and with not too much labour, at 4 feet – a good working height.

Much of the success and long life of a hedge is due to the original preparation of the soil. Most gardeners plant hedges 'forever', and so soil must be very well dug, well drained and enriched, especially with humus, for a hedge consists of a highly competitive community of plants, and one must ensure that enough good food exists for each plant to grow well.

Ordinary soil is suitable for most hedging plants and you will see by my lists that follow that there are many that will grow almost anywhere. But before planting be certain that the hedge you choose is suitable. Some plants – *Cupressus macrocarpa* comes quickly to my mind – will die in cold, wet soils.

The easiest way to prepare the site for a hedge is to use a line and to make a trench in which everything you can spare or afford in the way of humus that will benefit the plants can be incorporated. This is one case when double digging is necessary. This means removing the topsoil for a spade's depth and standing in the trench and forking over the bottom from one end to the other. Before forking, spread well-rotted animal manure, well-rotted garden compost, or leafmould in the trench. If none of these is available, buy some peat and mix it well with a general proprietary fertiliser or bonemeal.

Next, put most of the soil back into the trench but withhold some so that when the hedge is planted you can spread the roots out, cover them with the soil and firm them in well.

You may decide to plant a single or a double row of plants. There is no rule about this, except that if you plant a double row you should stagger the plants so that the one behind fills in the space between the two in front of it. A hedge can be planted quite close to a mesh fence. It is generally recommended that it should be planted 18 to 24 inches away from a wooden fence – but my advice is to allow a little more than this if you are likely (a) to trim it and (b) to use a powered trimmer. A foot and a half is not sufficient room to handle a machine easily and without causing damage.

Hedges may be planted at any time between September and May – the earlier the better, so that the plants can become really established before spring and can shoot anew naturally.

Hedges are planted for permanency so prepare the soil well and plant with care. Choose hedging plants which are proven to do well in your soil and situation for a mistake can be very expensive.

Evergreen hedges are best planted in early autumn or late spring. Cold winter planting does not suit them. Keep the plants well watered, foliage as well as roots.

If you want a clipped hedge, you should spend the first two or three years encouraging the hedge to 'feather' close to the ground. Do not let the plants grow too high too fast. Discourage this by keeping the top clipped so that new shoots are made at the base. Only when these are thick enough to suit you should you allow the hedge to grow upwards for a few inches. Clip this portion, too, until it is dense enough and then let it grow a little more. In the early years of a hedge the young plants need to be cut quite often. In the same way that you pinch out the centre of say, an antirrhinum, to make a nice bushy plant, so you keep cutting off the tips of a hedge plant to encourage it to become bushy.

It is natural for new gardeners to be in a hurry but it is a great mistake to try to rush the growth of a hedge. The fastest growers are often the shortest lived. Gaps caused by dead bushes take time and trouble to fill.

Even where the hedge is intended to form a windbreak the young plants themselves must be protected from wind until they are firmly anchored and growing well.

If you feel that the hedge is encroaching too much in width, then it may be kept cut back and so kept under control. This is best done with secateurs and if you have a lot of hedge this can be a lengthy job. This is something to be borne in mind when selecting the hedge plant.

Informal hedges will not need to be so severely trained as the formal clipped kinds. As with most other things in life, hedge distinctions are not always clear cut. However, a formal hedge is one which at some time or another is trimmed closely with shears or a powered hedge trimmer. Although they are kept strictly under control one should not assume they are cut often but they must be cut regularly. In some cases this means once a year only. Flowering and informal hedges are trimmed or cut by secateurs unless otherwise stated.

It is sometimes enough that an informal hedge is cut – carefully of course – for stems for flower arrangement. In this case one need not religiously observe the cutting dates, for obviously a continual, rather than a seasonal, supply of cut material is needed. But my advice is to distribute the cutting, taking a stem from here and there and not all in one place.

Times for clipping and cutting hedges are based on the seasons in which the plant involved makes its new growth. Unwise and untimely clipping can result in injury to the plant. What often happens is that young shoots are encouraged to grow at a time in the year when they become frosted. So it is important to observe trimming dates.

There are a few general rules. Newly planted hawthorn and privet should receive a first clipping in June, a second six weeks later in mid-July, and one more in September. After this, follow the dates given in catalogues under the description of each subject.

Not all hedges should be clipped with shears. Some plants look very ugly after being cut this way – the large-leaved laurels and holly are examples.

Throughout the book I use the term 'pruning' when secateurs are to be used, and 'clipping' when shears or a powered trimmer may be employed. Excessive trimming can damage or even kill a hedge. Certain evergreens, particularly conifers, are affected this way.

Not all hedges are intended as outer boundaries nor as dense screens. Generally speaking the hedges above 4 feet are for external boundaries or for large gardens. I believe that most gardeners will find more suitable hedges in the sections on informal types. Often hedges are used to divide one section of the garden from another. At other times their use is

Trimming a hedge with one of the wide range of powered tools now available for this purpose

purely decorative, in ways I have suggested in the chapters on design and planning. A low hedge can give the essential finish to certain parts or features of a garden. A walk or a path can be made prettier, even more romantic or intimate, if flanked by a hedge on one side or both.

Where a grassed or some other covered area joins a different part of the garden a low hedge, which need not necessarily be a straight one, makes a logical link. Where parts of the garden are of different heights, a low hedge helps to lead the eye along one level to another.

Such hedges can be formal and precisely clipped, the traditional yew 'walls' are examples, but informal types consisting of plants which demand the minimum of attention will relieve the gardener of a great deal of labour. These can be highly decorative and colourful.

Informal hedges can be very low, not much more than ground coverers, or they can be tall enough to block the view of the kitchen garden, shed or compost heap.

If you have only a small garden and if you really want your hedge for nothing more than a border between your plot and the next, think in terms of some pretty flowering plant which will help you decorate the house indoors as well as out.

Roses are ideal. Strong growers can be used as boundary hedges. If you keep pegging long trails down into the ground, the hedge will keep tidy and grow thick enough to keep animals out. Many of the shrub roses are ideal for this purpose. Zéphirine Drouhin is a thornless rose good for hedges.

Many of the hardy, vigorous, modern floribundas make wonderful hedges. We must not forget either that a flowering floribunda hedge is a continuous source of flowers for the home for many months of the year.

There are also many other types of roses that make good outer hedges and a keen rosarian would, on request, present you with a large list of roses, species, hybrids and varieties which would certainly be suitable for a hedge, but not all are labour-saving and certainly not all are suitable for the small garden. It is one thing to remove dead wood or to thin out in March, but another to have to remove limitless dead flowers during summer as well, a time when so much else calls for attention.

A rose hedge looks charming in association with some other plant growing as a low hedge before and below it. A good choice is one which retains its leaves all winter so that when the rose bushes are bare of foliage there will be some other plant to hold the interest. I recommend the silver- or grey-leaved shrubs such as lavender, santolina or senecio. If these silver bushes are allowed to bloom there is the extra value of summer colour. Sometimes tall-growing roses are planted with a dwarfer form before them.

There must be many gardeners at the seaside. Those who live in coastal areas do have particular problems as well as advantages. The greatest enemy is wind, which is not only strong but also salt-laden and causes plants, evergreens in particular, to become burned. On the other hand, coastal districts are warmer in winter than inland. For this reason, many tender or not quite hardy plants can be grown in sheltered gardens.

Obviously hedges are of great importance for shelter, and often not one, but several, are essential according to the design of the garden. Generally I believe that some boundary other than a hedge is best, for this can be built on the side of the prevailing wind and in its lea many attractive plants can be grown. In small gardens a windbreak of something other than plant material can be established, while to make it more decorative one of the suitable trees may be planted near it.

In windy places and near the sea there are many silver-leaved plants such as *Senecio greyii* with yellow daisies, or the herb, rosemary, which will flourish. The shrubby veronicas will give you flowers in autumn and late summer. Veronica is evergreen and prettily flowered. There are variegated forms suitable for small gardens and which grow well near the sea. So do euonymus and *Fuchsia magellanica riccartonii*. *Olearia haastii*, which becomes smothered with blossom and truly earns its name daisy bush, will grow anywhere. Various types of berberis are good and pretty in spring and autumn. Escallonia is evergreen and blooms in the summer.

A hedge of lavender is often just the thing to divide a flower garden. If you can raise the soil and plant the bushes on top of a ridge, a bank or a wall it will do even better for lavender is naturally a seaside plant and likes a sunny exposed situation. It resists the wind wonderfully well; its thin leaves are designed just for this purpose.

Paving the way

We all need the means of getting dry-foot from one part of the garden to another, and if we don't take care this can be a very expensive item in both time and money. On the other hand, if you choose carefully your paths can add greatly to the beauty of your garden.

Once chosen, a path can be made gradually without a great deal of inconvenience. It will almost inevitably begin from the house, so this is the section to make first. Unless you are on virtually stoneless ground, its foundation can be made in stages from stones collected as you prepare the garden elsewhere, otherwise you must import this hard core.

Aim for a width of at least 2 feet. If you try to keep it narrower than this, you may stumble – it is surprisingly easy to do so. You may also damage plants growing at the side. Four feet is a better width if you have to push wheelbarrows, mowers or the children's tricycles along it.

The summer cypress or burning bush, *Kochia trichophylla*, is a hardy annual which rapidly grows to form a perfect bush 2 to 3 feet high. In autumn the attractive, finely cut foliage turns a lovely coppery crimson. Here it is grown with yellow and pink petunias which will produce their lovely, trumpet-shaped flowers all summer

A path that has a border of tall plants on one side and dwarf plants or lawn on the other may safely be narrower than one which passes through tall plants. A garden looks prettier if plants are allowed to spill over the edges of a path so allow room for this.

The simplest way through a garden is the stepping-stone type of path where the stones are laid flush with the level of the soil. Stepping-stones may be laid on grass, a fraction below the level so that the mower can safely pass over them. Flag stones, pavement stones, Cotswold roof tiles and cement squares may all be used.

A path which is to be surfaced must be dug out. First mark it with canes or pegs of wood. Take out the soil to a depth of about nine inches or a foot (a spit deep). Save the good soil to use elsewhere in the garden. Fill the dug area half full of builder's rubble, clinkers or stones. All these will help to drain the soil on either side of the path. Make sure that this drainage layer is level. Test by laying a length of wood across. A test with a spirit level is even better and more accurate.

Over this layer you need to lay ashes and ideally a two-inch layer of builder's sand or gravel. On this you can rest your paving, building it up or scraping it away to ensure an even and level surface.

Try to make the edges fit as tightly together as you can. Scatter sand over the surface of the paving and with a hard brush sweep it between all the crevices. It will bind the paving together.

Paving varies from flagstone paving, random paving, random paving with a straight and uniform edge, crazy paving, cobble paving, crazy and cobble combined and brick on its own or with something else. In fact there are unlimited opportunities.

Crazy paving is a mixture of irregular-shaped pieces of stone of the same kind and roughly equal thickness, usually 1 to 2 inches.

Random is rectangular pieces of varied stone, all with right angled corners. Local paving can often be bought, usually 1½ to 2 inches thick. One ton covers roughly 10 to 12 square yards of surface. There are many good coloured cement paving stones made by various firms.

But paving stones, of whatever kind and shape, are not the only materials available to us for paths. There are gravel, ashes, cement, bitumen or plain soil. Whatever material is used, however, the basic groundwork or the foundation should be the same in order to get the best results.

Gravel is usually sold by the cubic yard. This will cover 12 to 18 square yards at about 2 to 3 inches thick. It should be raked evenly over the surface and rolled several times to make it even and compacted.

Ashes can frequently be obtained from local gasworks. These should be treated in exactly the same way as gravel.

A cement path is unquestionably the longest lasting. But it is heavy, difficult and time-taking to lay oneself. Neither is it particularly attractive, with its hard lines, although these can be softened by growing low-lying plants at the edges. Cement or concrete paths can be made in different colours.

Newcomers to the paving field in this country are the cold-laid bitumen surfaces. These come in a plastic sack and are tipped out on the prepared area, raked level and rolled. Coloured chips are scattered on the surface to break up the otherwise black or brown colour. This material hardens in a matter of a day or two and gives a neat, trouble free surface.

The best way of weeding paths is to use a weed-killer which can be sprayed on with a watering-can. It will last for about a year and will not spread to adjoining flower beds or grass. See page 62.

You can see that there is a great choice of path surfaces – certainly enough to allow originality in design as well as ease in construction. A pleasant path surface I have admired in other people's gardens is raked sand. Where there is likely to be a great deal of traffic, this is used with flag, brick, tile or even a stepping-stone path as a margin on each side. Raking can be no more than keeping the surface level, but on the other hand it is quite easy by manipulating the rake to scratch an attractive pattern on the surface, though this needs to be done frequently. There can be a pleasing play of colour tones here, as well as textures, according to the type of sand and paving used.

Change of texture is fortunately a simple matter. Where, for example, we were advocating a stepping-stone path either as a permanent or a temporary means of getting from one place to another, the spaces between the stones could well be filled with consolidated garden rubble. A comparable – though more attractive and durable – effect can be obtained by inserting large, round pebbles into wet concrete, leaving them just proud of the cement. Another method of obtaining contrast in texture is to brush the surface of a wet concrete block to leave the aggregate just showing, or again to lay blocks so that the 'grain' of the tamping goes from north to south in one block and from east to west in its neighbour. Defined patterns can be scratched or pegged out. On one pavement I saw, large pavement flags (bought cheaply at the local town council's yard) had been laid down as the main fabric of the

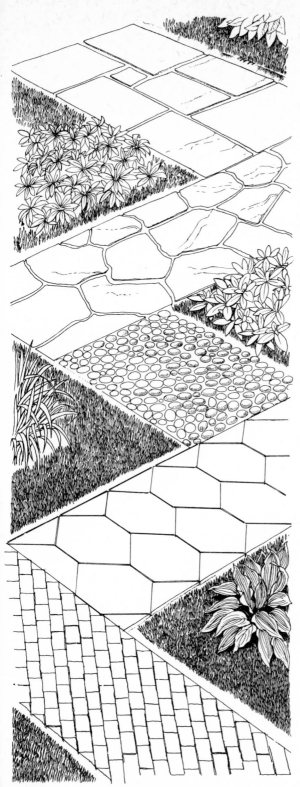

The right choice of paving material, well laid on a solid foundation, will greatly enhance your garden

paving but no attempt had been made to fit the stone edges flush with the borders. Instead, the geometrically shaped spaces had been filled with a contrasting small stone. Make sure that your textures really do contrast. Paving and gravel or pebbles will look better than pebbles and gravel chips.

Since we all know that grass covers soil surface so efficiently, don't disregard it as 'paving'. Actually the contrast (or perhaps 'association' would be a better word) of grass and stone is very pleasant as you may have observed if you have seen some continental gardens in which large cobble stones are margined by grass sown between them.

This pattern of green and stone colour is a pleasant one, as you would expect of such a natural association. In a country garden or some other place where the surface thus covered is subjected to much traffic, you need not be too meticulous about keeping the grass shorn. However, it can easily be kept short by using a mower with the blades set high. Weeds can be kept under control by the use of selective weedkillers.

Plants other than grass can also be used for this purpose; for example, close-growing thymes and dwarf periwinkle. Their selection will really depend upon where this area is and the amount of traffic to which it is likely to be subjected. Beware they do not become slippery.

This style of paving can be used as a pattern within a pattern. If, for example, the area around a tree is to be paved, perhaps because a seat is to be built round the tree or because it stands in an area to be covered, a circle of grass and stone over the tree roots can be bordered by plain paving. Generally speaking, a circular pattern is more pleasing than a rectangular one, though a diamond is often attractive and a star is lovely.

Alternatively, you can graduate the textures, lead in gently, one to the other by placing grass and stone next to the lawn with pure stone of some kind in the central area.

The shape of a path is as important as the shape of a border. There may be occasions when all must have straight lines because of the proportions and designs of the house, but often a meandering path will be more pleasing. This is a personal decision.

The drive to the garage is often overlooked, and yet there is so much of it that it should be taken in as part of the garden plan. Quite often the wall of the garage is a continuation of the wall or fence dividing the one garden from that of next door. This area directly below the fence can be made useful and

attractive. A raised bed, or a slightly raised bed gives one the opportunity of making an attractive stone edging and ensures that the plants are neither driven nor trodden upon. Along a fence of this kind, according to its aspect, one can grow evergreens, such as cotoneaster or camellias (in which case the raised bed can have a good supply of peat added), fruiting cordon or fan-shaped trees such as Morello cherry if on the north – lovely in blossom-time – peaches, apricots and nectarines on the south and west, apples, pears, or even a grape vine if the fence is warm enough.

The approach to the garage is usually concreted and so often is ugly, arid and too hot in summer. How much better to concrete the wheel-ways and to pattern the area on either side. I have seen garage drives in which the area between the wheel-ways is planted with low-growing ground cover plants, such as sweet-smelling thyme, and low-growing annuals.

Colour when you need it most

Judging by the hundreds of letters which reach me all gardeners have one dream, one aim, to which they direct the bulk of their labours. It comes as a plea, sometimes I feel, almost as a cry from the heart, 'How can I plan my garden so that I can find something in flower every day of the year?' It's not as difficult as it sounds.

Many shrubs begin producing their flowers in October and November. After this time everything depends upon the weather. In prolonged snow and frost no plant can be expected to produce masses of frail flowers. But many will open in spite of normal cold days and winds. Low-growing shrubs such as heathers will actually go on growing and blooming under snow. One winter when the thaw came at last we were overjoyed to see *Erica carnea* bright pink with flowers, prettily exposed as the snow retreated from the plant.

Erica carnea differs from most ericaceous plants in that it will tolerate a little lime but the emphasis must be on *little*. A chalk soil, for instance, is too limy.

Generally speaking ericas bloom for three months.

E. darleyensis is a winter-flowering hybrid I warmly recommend, a cross between *E. carnea* and *E. mediterranea*. It grows nearly 2 feet and flowers from November to April.

Larger forms of heathers include *E. arborea*, the tree heath, which will grow to 10 feet or more and *E. mediterranea* from 4 to 10 feet. Flowers of the first appear in January, continue to March and are followed by those of the second which continue to May.

A charming member of the erica family is *Leucothoë catesbaei*, an evergreen shrub that will grow as high as 6 feet. The slender arching branches on which small white flowers are borne in long rows of short racemes are graceful for winter flower arrangement. There are also *L. davisiae*, evergreen, and a good

Hydrangeas are so easy to grow and so universally planted in gardens that we tend to take them for granted. This close-up of the flowers of the lacecap *Hydrangea macrophylla serrata*, a charming small shrub, shows, however, just how beautiful they can be. There are very many species and varieties to choose from

deciduous species, *L. racemosa*. They enjoy a light peaty soil and dislike lime.

Much depends on the shelter available to the plants. A warm wall or a warm corner made by walls at right angles will protect and even force certain plants into early bloom. However, and as one might expect, many winter-flowering shrubs and climbers do well on the north side of a house. Camellias for example, so long as they are not constantly nipped by wind, have glossier leaves when growing in this aspect than elsewhere.

Camellias are much hardier than many people realise. I have heard of them standing 24 degrees of frost. In January, *C. nobilissima* produces its white flowers in enough quantity to be useful for cutting. This camellia never drops when cut like some of the 'bad openers'. The flowers turn yellow, but not unpleasantly, with frost. They continue until March. I know of a home where *C. nobilissima* has been on the Christmas table three years running!

The *williamsii* strain of these plants, single and semi-double, is known as perpetual flowering, blooming as it does from January to April.

If you buy a camellia in a pot or container you can plant it at any time but it is most important to get the soil in the correct condition. Camellias will grow well in neutral but not in alkaline soil. They prefer an acid one. The ideal pH is about 5·0. They will also flourish in heavy soils. The best fertiliser is bonemeal, 14 pounds mixed with 1 hundredweight of peat and used as a topdressing.

Few plants are as spectacular as the forsythia in bloom. *F. intermedia spectabilis*, the earliest form to be introduced into cultivation, is still the best although there is a wider choice today. It grows up to 10 feet tall and flowers in March and April.

Forsythia suspensa, usually grown supported as a climber, will grow to 10 feet. If it is kept under control it is most graceful with its pendulous branches and large bright yellow flowers.

They are easy plants to grow, careless of soil type, free from pests, quick to develop and rewarding with bloom.

Viburnums are shrubs for all gardens. Many of them flower through winter and are very fragrant. Possibly the best known is *V. tinus*. This species though is not as fragrant as the others. *V. carlesii* is one of the most sweetly scented of all plants and flowers in April. *V.* Park Farm Hybrid flowers much earlier but is not so scented. *V. macrocephalum* is not very hardy and should be grown in sheltered gardens. It has green flowers which change to pure white as they mature in March.

Probably earliest of all viburnums is the hybrid *V. bodnantense* Dawn, which produces its arching pink flower sprays for Christmas and carries them until the end of February.

Not all colour comes from flowers. Many berried shrubs continue to be showy throughout the shortest days. Cotoneasters are lovely in December and January. *C. cornubia* is a lovely shrub. *C. salicifolia* is daintier and generally of a lighter habit with smaller berries. They are excellent for cutting.

Of course, berried shrubs provide food for the birds which will descend on them once the weather becomes really bad, but *Pyracantha angustifolia* is not a favourite with them. Unlike other pyracanthas, the berries remain on this one until the end of March.

A most obliging shrub is the skimmia. Unfortunately, its nomenclature seems to be in a bit of a muddle and not all nurserymen agree. The true *foremanii* keeps its berries on all the year but it is unlikely that you can buy the true one. However, other skimmias are good value too.

Evergreens are especially valuable because they furnish the garden so attractively always.

Magnolias have the magic exotic appearance that is certain to bring any hardy plant popularity. There are many suitable for small and large gardens. Recently I saw a tall tree, *M. kobus*, which had been grown from seed sown 14 years ago. This is an extremely dainty species with pure white flowers in March and April.

Many magnolias can be treated either as trees or shrubs, depending on the space available. They like an acid soil and don't like to be disturbed, so plant them early in their permanent home and leave them alone.

Perhaps the best known is *M. soulangeana*, flowering when quite a small shrub but growing to 20 feet and producing white flowers with a purple exterior from April to June.

A fairly new hybrid, an accidental cross at Kew gardens between *M. kobus* and *M. salicifolia*, is *M. kewensis*. It has been widely praised and has received several awards. It produces large, white, scented flowers when comparatively young and is normally free from frost damage.

Good for a small garden is *M. salicifolia*, the willow-leaved magnolia. It makes a slender tree, producing white flowers in April before the leaves appear. The bark is scented and said to smell like verbena.

Some plants that have neither leaf nor flower in winter are still highly decorative because of the colour of the bark. Yellow and red dogwood planted near each other are such a delight, the two hues complementing each other so attractively. Botanical names are *Cornus alba atrosanguinea* (red) and *C. stolonifera flaviramea* (yellow). They grow in ordinary soils but do perhaps best if it is slightly acid.

Similar in effect are some of the willows. We grow two groups for their stem colour alone, which glows out against the green of conifers in the dark days. *Salix vitellina* has bright yellow shoots, *S. v. britzensis* bright red.

Both dogwood and willows will grow into quite tall trees if left alone, but in this condition they lose most of their bright winter colour. Cut almost to the ground in March each year they quickly send up vividly coloured shoots. This makes them ideal for small gardens.

Among the climbers *Clematis armandii*, with white flowers tipped with pink and foliage similar to a passion flower, will bloom in March or early April. It should be pruned immediately after flowering. Give it a warm wall to grow on and some protection against winter frosts. Even earlier is *C. calycina*, which produces its creamy white freckled flowers in January and February. This, too, needs protection from frost.

Cherries or prunus are the first trees to bloom, often in early March, and the first to colour in the autumn.

No garden should be without at least one winter-flowering prunus. We have a *P. subhirtella autumnalis* with the small delicately pinked flower petals of a soft rose. It begins to flower in November and we like always to have a few sprigs with other blossom on the Christmas table.

There are a surprising number of types of *Prunus subhirtella*. All are good trees for the small garden.

Cherries are accommodating plants. They do well on chalk or on rhododendron soil! All the same, the area for the tree must be well prepared and enriched because too much lime sometimes causes chlorosis, a yellowing of leaves and other deficiencies. What they must have is good drainage. Incidentally, when buying a cherry always ask for one that has been 'budded' or grafted at the base. This portion of the tree swells and is often very ugly. If it is at the base of the tree instead of at the top of the trunk it can be hidden. If buds from the stock occur at this point they can be rubbed off. (Remove buds and suckers from grafted trees.)

Other recommended cherries are *P. Beni Higan Sakura* with early pale pink flowers; *P. yedoensis* which becomes completely smothered in pure white blossom in March, but alas, its season is short – only about ten days – and so it is an extravagance unless you have a lot of room; *P. pandora*, a foam of soft pink in March, is an excellent tree for a small garden. *P. cantabrigiensis* is one of the earliest, given a sheltered spot.

Prunus incisa praecox is a white-blossomed winter-flowering plum. This prunus, *P. communis* (the almond), and the peach, *P. persica*, will grow in town and country alike.

There are enough winter- and early-spring-flowering rhododendrons to suit everyone's taste. Just remember that the more hairs there are on a rhododendron, the less hardy it is, so buy smooth glossy types.

Rhododendron Christmas Cheer really does flower at Christmas! Pick it when the buds are just showing colour and remove some of the leaves if you want it for home decoration. *R. shilsonii*, a vivid red, is probably the most outstanding of early rhododendrons. For rock gardens, there is *R. repens* with waxy red bells about the size of a gentian. Another hybrid is *R. Moonshine* from which came the best strain of hardy hybrid yellow rhododendrons.

Others than the winter types bloom from the end of April through May and the very late, from June to July.

Azaleas and rhododendrons are the same plant botanically, but there are deciduous (often colouring beautifully in autumn) as well as evergreen azaleas and generally they are much smaller. They are ideal for the small garden. Most azaleas favour the yellow, orange and apricot colour range, though there are some new varieties which are in soft pinks and mauves.

The hardiest of all rhododendrons is the purple species you have probably seen growing wild, *R. ponticum*. Its counterpart in the azalea world is *A. ponticum*. *Ponticum* means coming from the shores of the Black Sea! This has bright yellow flowers which are strongly scented and instead of being evergreen has brilliant autumn foliage.

If you have neutral or peaty soil all of these will grow happily. They look their best grown together. One can grow certain bulbs including lilies with them. The soil beneath them can be carpeted with heathers, bilberries or the delightful creeping dogwood, *Cornus canadensis*. These plants will grow under the shade of trees or at the edge of light woodland. They make a delightful link between wild and formal gardens. On the other hand rhododendrons will flourish in full sun so long as their roots are kept cool and comparatively moist. Peat mulches are good.

The cherry-coloured flowering currant, *Ribes sanguineum*, can be seen in most cottage gardens (I have even seen a clipped hedge of it) and can be cut to force indoors as soon as its flower buds become plump. There is a lovely white variety, *album*, the racemes of which are long and graceful.

The odd but titillatingly scented witch hazels (hamamelis) will bloom in a sheltered place even though snow lies all around. In summer they are not much to rave about – rather like a gross hazel nut bush – but in mid-winter and onwards the branches become decorated with yellow tassels. There are many varieties of varying hues. *Hamamelis mollis pallida* is a pleasant sulphur yellow.

What many winter-flowering shrubs lack in glory they make up for in fragrance. A favourite cottage garden shrub is the little daphne. These prefer a sandy, peaty soil and are apt to die off in limy soils. *D. laureola* with scented yellow-green flowers is uncommon and flowers in February and March. The tiny white *D. blagayana* blooms in March and April; *D. collina,* purple-rose, from May to June.

Many of the maples or acers provide foliage colour and some of them go on to give us bark colour that can be seen brilliantly right down the garden.

There is the vivid liquidambar, afire with brilliant foliage, the parrotia, hamamelis, fothergilla, rhus, sorbus and many more, a wide collection which enriches and obliges us with splendid summer foliage ending in a firework display of brilliant colour at the end of the season when we most need it.

But even these leaves fall and while we are left with bare stems our eyes shift to the berries, some of which shine from evergreen foliage. We can choose berberis, crataegus, hollies, roses, the vines and snowberries to fit into the garden scheme.

Yet it is not only the true spectrum colours that serve us well in the dark days. White, silver and grey are increasingly important in our gardens. There are many grey- or silver-leaved plants in cultivation which can shine through the darkness of winter days. They range from santolina and artemisia through many of the dianthus and the hosta to the lavenders and olearias. Even some of the cupressus, pittosporum, populus and pyrus are useful in their season.

The rose as a shrub

We have become accustomed to treating roses strictly as plants for beds where we isolate them and where they thrive and look very lovely. I am not criticising this method for I grow many roses this way myself but I would like to put forward an idea (not a new one) that roses should also be considered as shrubs and allowed to grow their own way. The old-fashioned kinds and species, as well as some modern varieties are, in fact, often called shrub roses.

The species also have among them some very striking members ideal for gardens which have space for them, especially informal or wild gardens. The lovely *Rosa moyesii* has fabulous, dark red, velvety flowers but like so many of these species they are single and do not live so long as the full-petalled modern roses. It is possible to raise species roses from seed.

The tremendous number of variations and hybrids have resulted in so many names and so many forms that it is difficult without considerable study to define rose types accurately and I pity the poor amateur when I have so much difficulty myself! Even the definitive Royal Horticultural Society's *Dictionary of Gardening* remarks rather plaintively, 'in one recent classification no fewer than 48 classes are named and even then some groups which have distinctive horticultural characteristics are combined with others. So great a sub-division to a large extent defeats its own ends and rather tends to confuse than to clarify.' I agree!

The R.H.S. itself defines ten groups: Hybrid Tea,

The informal planting of roses in mixed flower beds especially those containing cottage garden perennials like lavender and nepeta can look very attractive and this treatment lends itself well to the smaller garden where the owner needs to make the most economical and decorative use of the space available to him

Hybrid Perpetual, China and Hybrid China, Tea-scented, Noisette, Dwarf Polyantha, Hybrid Polyantha, Hybrid Musk, Penzance Briars and Hybrid Wichuraianas.

The modern roses, hybrid teas and floribundas and those which Americans call grandifloras (the floribunda-type variety with great clusters of blooms as big as hybrid teas, such as Queen Elizabeth), usually do better on their own, not mixed with an assortment of plants, mostly because they dislike having the soil round their roots continually disturbed. This is one reason why bulbs which have to be lifted annually are not good mixers and should not be used to make rose beds colourful in spring. Any hoeing carried out in summer to keep weeds down should be shallow. I use a modern hoe, almost oval in shape, with knife-sharp serrated edges, which skims the surface only and which I find to be an efficient tool for this purpose.

The traditional planting time for roses is any time between November and early April; roses on sale in containers may be planted in the summer months even when they are in flower.

You should uncover the plants as soon as they arrive from the nursery. If you cannot plant them because the ground is frosted, or for some other reason, then store them in a frost-proof place. While you do this, keep the roots moist by wrapping a damp sack round them or pack them into boxes or other containers filled with moist peat and let them stay until the weather is more favourable.

Choose a sunny open position to plant your roses. They do not grow well under trees. But watch that they are protected from wind or they become rocked, which is not good for them.

Give the roses plenty of room. The bush types, including the polyantha and floribunda types as well as hybrid teas, should not be closer ever than 18 inches. You can give them a little more room if you wish. Climbers and ramblers need to be at least $2\frac{1}{2}$ feet apart. If you are going to plant standards among your rose bushes put the standards 4 to 5 feet apart. You can alternate a rose bush between them.

If you intend making a rose bed, begin preparing the soil in October if you can. Roses like a deep, rich and slightly heavy soil. Try to get some well-rotted animal manure and apply it generously. The ideal is 1 hundredweight of manure to roughly 8 square yards. Failing animal manure use rotted compost. If you can get only a little organic manure try to mulch with it annually. Add also 4 to 6 ounces of bonemeal to a square yard. If you are cutting the bed from a grass patch you can use the turves

you skim off the top. Bury them under the soil as you dig placing the grass side downwards. Do not use lime.

When you plant, spread the roots out well as directed for shrubs and, as for other shrubs, go round and firm well after winter gales and at other times during the year.

When you plant the bushes, you need to prune them more severely than you will later on when they become established. Cut the shoots back to within three 'eyes' of the base. This means three buds counted from ground level. It is not always easy to see that these are buds. Often they more resemble the eyes of a potato, hence their name. Usually the third bud or eye comes just a few inches above ground level. But it is worth going down to the first or the second bud to choose one which points outwards from the centre of the bush, even if this means cutting the stem very short. This will give you nicely shaped bushes later on, for the shoot will grow out the way the bud is pointing.

You need to cut all types of bush roses this way, hybrid teas, polyantha or floribunda roses. The two latter should be cut right back the first year, and then in later years cut to about half the length of the strong shoots. In all bushes always cut away any weak or dead wood. General principles: prune to keep the centre open, to get rid of dead and weak shoots, to keep growth within bounds and to preserve strength for the production of flowers.

For climbing roses it is best to remove any weak or unripe (soft) wood and trim the two or three longest shoots by about one-third their length. As a rule these plants come from the rose grower pruned ready for planting.

Ramblers should have the flowering wood removed nearly to the base after flowering in August. This will encourage new shoots to break from the bottom and these should be trained in position in the autumn. These new shoots will bear the flowers the following summer. Try to 'horizontalise' the growth of ramblers and climbers. This way they will bear more flowers. Train new shoots as horizontally as possible and if you have to take them up to a certain height, allow the top portion to run horizontally. When pruning climbers cut always to a bud pointing in the direction you wish the shoot to grow and tie in the shoot as soon as it reaches a convenient length.

Standard roses should be treated the same way as the bush type. Cut the shoots back to within 4 to 6 inches of the base of the graft, the spot where the bush joins the main stem.

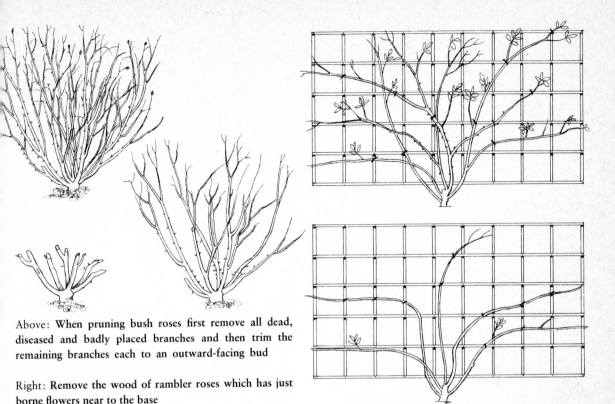

Above: **When pruning bush roses first remove all dead, diseased and badly placed branches and then trim the remaining branches each to an outward-facing bud**

Right: **Remove the wood of rambler roses which has just borne flowers near to the base**

The main rose pruning is done in March, but there are some roses that can receive attention through the winter. All those we call perpetual flowering (those that continue flowering as long as they possibly can), bourbon, hybrid musk, noisette, rugosa, hybrid perpetual and hybrid tea, should have the flowering stems cut away so that they are encouraged to keep on growing.

The most important thing with roses is to see that their roots are cool and that there is food easily available. The second is to see that the plants do not suffer from pests and predators but that the foliage and flowers continue to grow, the leaves glossy with health. The third is that all faded flowers should be constantly removed, incidentally a form of pruning which everyone can understand. All these essentials are easy to ensure.

We must realise that if our roses are ill, one of the reasons is our method of growing them. We're not looking after them properly! Good feeding, a protective mulch of grass clippings, or some other material, careful destruction of diseased prunings, proper pruning at the right time, all these will give you much cleaner plants and better blooms. When you feed, remember that too much nitrogen will give lush, tender and susceptible growth, so encourage strong healthy growth with a spring dressing of sulphate of potash, 3 ounces to a square yard.

The classic rose fertiliser (Tonk's) is obtainable made up from most garden stores or can be mixed yourself from: (by weight) 10 parts nitrate of potash, 12 parts superphosphate of lime, 2 parts sulphate of magnesium, one part sulphate of iron and 8 parts sulphate of lime. Apply in April at 4 ounces per square yard. Several fertiliser firms have prepared their own specialised rose feeds, largely based on this formula but sometimes containing additional materials. Basic balanced fertilisers are almost as good and will save you money. If you feed thoroughly and correctly in the spring, don't bother again unless you are growing for exhibition. If you've been less enthusiastic, a normal garden fertiliser two or three times throughout the summer will keep the plants growing and flourishing.

The main pests of roses are aphids, thrips and caterpillars; the main diseases are mildew, black spot and rust. Two types of spray can control all these: insecticides such as BHC and malathion and fungicides such as sulphur, zineb and captan. Some can even be mixed to give complete control in a single spray. There are now systemic insecticides and fungicides, both giving long-term protection. Remember, always follow the manufacturer's instructions when using these chemicals.

Blessed shade

A garden without shade is a garden without peace. So try to make shade for your own benefit, as well as for the plants. Do not think that the choice of plants is restricted or that a shady plot can never be as pretty as one that lies in the sun. Even in deep shade there are many plants that can be grown and enjoyed. Few of them ever reach the brilliance of those in the sunny border – for example only few flowering annuals do well – but all of them are plants of great character. You can be recompensed by lovely colour from bulbous plants in spring. Since most are perennials they may be left undisturbed, sometimes for years. Some of them, like polygonatum or Solomon's seal, are rhizomatous and should not be disturbed or they will disappear.

None are so co-operative as ferns, which grow in the shadiest of corners. The list of hardy ferns is much longer than many laymen realise. There are fern specialists who carry a selection from those to grow in walls like the asplenium to *Onoclea sensibilis* which will tolerate a wet position and even a few inches of water. Generally speaking, the environment that suits ferns best is partially shady, slightly moist and cool. There are some suitable for dry spots, too, and some are evergreen.

Because they need so little light, all spring-flowering bulbs grow anywhere in the shade, but there are others which bloom at other times of the year also. Some of these like the schizostylis give wonderful colours in late autumn.

Most plants that enjoy shade like their conditions to be moist and the soil rich. Yet we find that though plants adapt themselves surprisingly well to different types of soil in spite of their natural inclinations (no doubt the fallen leaves under trees help provide a correct root hold for plants which grow there), they are less likely to fit into a shady garden if they like sun and vice versa. There are a few that grow in both sun or part shade.

Possibly, what most affects plants grown in the shade of trees or buildings is the amount of drip to which they are subjected. A few, like hostas, revel in it, but others die. There are other plants, but only a few, that will tolerate any situation. Where ground is waterlogged, it is well worthwhile installing an efficient drainage system. If open soil is then placed above the drain a greater variety of plants may be grown than before.

In their natural surroundings we can see wild herbaceous, bulbous and shrubby plants alike growing close to the foot of the trunk of many types of tree; sometimes, as in the case of the polypody fern, actually growing on the trunk and along some of the larger limbs. (A good nature tip for those who want to clothe a rotting stump.) In some woods the ground cover is thick, for many plants grow well and increase in the humus-rich, moist leafmould. In our gardens we have to search and experiment to find what plants get along well together.

So many shrubs grow prettily in shade. A few will tolerate dark corners but most like half shade, by which we mean not only the dappled protection of nearby trees but the coolness cast by long shadows at different times of the day.

Although we often see hydrangeas in open sunny places, the ideal position for them is in a sheltered semi-shaded place. These plants do not like drips from trees. In shade their blooms are deeper hues than when they grow in the open. *H. petiolaris,* the climbing species, can be allowed to scramble along the ground. This is a species that will grow on a north site and like other shrubs that dwell in this position it will grow in shade.

For quick ground coverers, try sprawlers. These are plants such as winter jasmine that are usually supported. They can be allowed to run along the ground and then trained up a tree if liked.

One can introduce colour to shady spots by training climbers – clematis in particular – but also polygonum and some roses to climb trees or to top fences and walls. This is an attractive way of getting the effect of colour from a distance.

Some trees do present a problem. For example, you will find few plants growing beneath beech trees. So avoid planting beech unless the trees can be grown as specimens on lawns; (wood meadow grass, *Poa nemoralis,* grows well under trees). If you have inherited a beech tree, underplant it liberally with *Cyclamen neapolitanum,* which will do very well. Plant the corms in early autumn. Squirrels go for them, so in the early stages cover the planted area with small-mesh wire-netting. The delightful little

Rhododendrons and bluebells make excellent companions in a wild garden or a shady corner for they thrive under the same conditions. The rhododendron here is the variety Lady Chamberlain which is one of the loveliest grown in gardens although it is only fully hardy in warm, sheltered situations. The bluebell is *Endymion non-scriptus*

flowers will cover the ground from August to October and after them the beautifully marked leaves will make a pretty carpet. Other hardy cyclamen can be planted round the perimeter of the shade with early spring flowers.

For those who have made shrubberies, shade-loving 'cover' plants are essential not only to keep down weeds but also to provide the ecological balance necessary. There are many perennials suitable, but some biennials are also good and very showy. These can be left to seed themselves. Myosotis or forget-me-not is one of the most effective, and will grow well among shrubs because it is dwarf. Honesty, with purple flowers in spring and silver 'moons' in winter, looks lovely among taller trees. So do the foxgloves. Small spring flowers such as crocus species, chionodoxa and *Scilla sibirica* will become naturalised and seed themselves.

The most important thing to decide before choosing plants, no matter what the cause of the shade, is whether the soil is constantly moist or dry.

Where the soil is dry (not to be confused with summer hard-baked soil, which is the result of waterlogging in winter) there are a few good herbaceous and shrubby ground cover plants that can quickly and easily become established. Some retain their leaves throughout the winter. These include anaphalis, bergenia, epimedium, saxifraga and vinca. Some others retain some foliage but are at their best from late spring onwards. These include aquilegia, especially the old-fashioned 'granny bonnets', asperula, campanula, digitalis, geranium (the herbaceous geranium or crane's-bill, not the potted types which are correctly pelargoniums), hypericum, lamium, mertensia, pachysandra, polygonum and symphytum. Most of these will do equally well, perhaps even better, in a moist place.

For moist woodland conditions the list is much longer and contains some very interesting plants. Not many are true evergreens but most have distinctive foliage which appears early in the season and persists with the very severe weather. The list contains the few all-rounders I mentioned in the list for dry shade plants.

Bulbs for ground cover

To appreciate the value of ground cover plants one must forget the over-groomed garden with its several square inches of weed-free soil round every plant, and consider instead the ways of nature. In a meadow every bit of soil is covered, yet there is a tremendous variety of plants. In lightly dappled copses or at the edges of dense forest, plants carpet the ground.

If ground cover plants are to be successful and play their part well, they must have a chance to become established without competing with weeds. Fortunately, there are now safe weedkillers which can be applied before planting or (and this I think is a more satisfactory method) you can apply mulches and composts as much as possible during the early days to prevent weeds colonising the area.

All ground cover plants can be planted within a few inches of the base of a shrub. After a time, they seem to snuggle up closer and this does not appear to have any bad effect. Where very young, and consequently small, shrubs are to be planted, these should be allowed to become established and really growing well before ground cover plants are planted quite close to them. Mulch the soil instead. When the time comes to plant the ground coverers, you might be able to divide those you already have. You can propagate from them in readiness for future planting.

Among the many lovely plants that cover the ground with drifts of flowers, we must include those which grow from bulbs.

Since bluebells, *Endymion non-scriptus* (sometimes still known as *Scilla nutans*), are so familiar to many of us as a natural floral carpet, let us consider others of this tribe which can be introduced with such charming effect into our gardens.

Most like the wild bluebell in appearance is *Endymion hispanicus* of which there are blue, white and pink varieties, and now many hybrids in lovely soft hues. These flower at about the same time as the bluebell. Showing colour much earlier than these, are *Scilla sibirica,* much dwarfer and with a divided corona, not a bell, and *S. bifolia,* similar but flowering earlier.

All these bulbs, and many others, do well so long as you let them grow undisturbed and allow them to seed freely. They may be bought by the dozen, hundred or thousand and are reasonably priced. How close you plant them will depend upon your pocket but, obviously, the more you can plant to begin with, the quicker the ground will become carpeted. It is possible, by planning, to grow a variety of plants from easily planted tubers, corms and bulbs so that one gets a succession of flowers from February (or earlier) to June.

The greatest asset of spring- and autumn-flowering bulbs is their willingness to grow beneath trees or in other situations where there is little direct sunlight. One can plant *Colchicum autumnale* (meadow saffron) which will grow even in dry soil. The lovely flowers, sometimes called 'naked ladies', appear in autumn and are followed by large handsome leaves which cover the soil in spring and die down in June and July.

Eranthis hyemalis, the winter aconite, 3 or 4 inches tall, flowers from January to March, according to its situation or the season, and will grow quite happily with snowdrops. These bulbs should be planted in groups near each other so that the groups merge one into the other, rather than singly so that individuals are mixed together in one area.

Also belonging to the same family, the *Ranunculaceae,* are the wind flowers or anemones, one species of which, *Anemone nemorosa,* carpets our woodlands in spring and which can also be coaxed to grow in gardens. Others, for planting under trees and in partial shade, are *A. apennina* and *A. blanda,* 6 inches, both in varied soft hues of blue, white and rose, blooming from February to April. All should be allowed to seed freely.

In our woods the white wood sorrel, *Oxalis acetosella,* said to be the true shamrock, flowers in spring. There is also a variety, *O. a. rosea.* This, too, can be used as ground cover in gardens, especially under high trees. (Another, *O. corniculata,* can be a troublesome weed.) A species from Chile, *O. adenophylla,* is a pretty purple-rose.

Many people choose narcissi and these really do look beautiful growing in grass and under trees. An orchard with fruit trees in bloom and daffodils below the branches is a wonderful sight. The objection to the hybrid narcissi is that they tend to deteriorate after some years, and the clumps must be lifted and divided. After this the bulbs recover and begin producing flowers again. This deterioration does not appear to occur with the species.

Among the most delightful of the small narcissi is *Narcissus cyclamineus.* This species is supposed to prefer moist situations, yet at the Royal Horticultural Society's Wisley Garden you can see them growing in dry places also. The late Francis Hanger, the curator, explained to me why this was so. He said that bulbs planted in a dry place will not do well but seed will grow, and those flourishing on the dry banks have been raised from seed.

There are other species, such as the tiny hoop petticoat daffodil, *N. bulbocodium,* which will grow prettily in natural surroundings, and so does our native wild daffodil, *N. pseudo-narcissus.*

Bulbs are the easiest and most rewarding of all flowers to grow. They will do well in any soil provided it is well drained. They will flower beautifully even in a brand new garden. Bulbs can be grown anywhere in the garden, in beds by themselves or mixed with shorter-growing flowers, such as tulips towering above forget-me-nots; in parts of borders, along edges, among shrubs, on rock gardens, naturalised in orchards and woodland, on lawns and between paving stones or in tubs or window-boxes. Spring-flowering bulbs do not need full sun.

It is advisable to lighten heavy soils with peat or well-rotted leafmould forked in. A little bonemeal, 3 to 4 ounces a square yard, is also beneficial. Plant the bulbs before frost hardens the ground. The planting period for spring-flowering bulbs usually extends from 1st September to 15th December, but daffodils and all other narcissi should be planted before the end of October. All bulbs should be planted pointed end up, 5 to 6 inches deep for daffodils, tulips and hyacinths; 3 to 4 inches deep for crocuses, muscari and most other small bulbs. Variation in depth depends on the size of the bulb and on the type of soil – the bigger the bulb and the lighter the soil, the deeper the planting.

The easiest way of planting naturalised bulbs is with a special tool known as a bulb planter. This cuts out a core of turf when it is pushed into the ground and removes it intact. The bulb can then be placed firmly in the hole and the core of turf replaced and firmed with the feet. Naturalised bulbs must be planted in drifts and not in rigid rows or clumps. To achieve a natural effect scatter the bulbs by hand and plant them where they fall. Over a period of years the bulbs will multiply and colonise the ground.

Water gardens

It takes a lot of labour to build, but once that's done, a water garden is not only charming and interesting but also labour-saving. Anyone who is getting on and finds gardening an effort might do well to consider making a formal rectangular pool the most important part of the garden. If the surround is paved to ensure easy walking and to avoid grass cutting, then labour has been cut almost to the limit. Such a garden can be made as part of a patio. A few beds, perhaps no larger than a paving slab can take shrubs or perennials.

At one time making a pond was sheer hard labour. Not only had the area to be excavated but also to be lined with concrete. And although this method is still a good one, there are now far easier ways of making water gardens and not only are the ways easier but the results are often more effective.

Once the hole has been dug (this is by far the longest and heaviest part of the job) you can make a water garden in a day.

There are three main types of plastics which replace the backbreaking time-and-money-consuming business of lining the pool with concrete. The least expensive is to line the interior of the pool with plastic sheeting. This can be clear, black, blue or stone coloured, or pebble patterned also. If possible the plastic should be laid on a bed of sand or peat so that no sharp stones can break through it. Cover the whole of the area and allow a foot or so overlap at the edges. The plastic sheeting must be smoothed over the bottom of the pool so that no wrinkles show and the overlap at the top should be weighted down with a little soil and then a stone edging, which should reach just an inch or two over the edge. Once all the wrinkles are smoothed away, the water can be let in.

The next method is very much the same except that the plastic sheeting is much thicker, tougher and more elastic. Some specialist firms make up special sizes so they fit exactly, even to making a ledge for little plants. This tougher sheeting will stretch, which means that it merely has to be fitted over the hole and when the water flows in, it stretches and fills the cavity exactly, the water pushing out all the wrinkles.

The easiest pools of all are those prefabricated in fibreglass. These come in several different shapes and sizes and all you have to do is to dig out the hole to fit the shape exactly and then drop in the pool, making quite sure that it is level. This type of pool will last almost indefinitely and maintains easily.

One of the greatest virtues of water in the garden is that it moves. Even the most sheltered pool on the stillest of days shows some shimmering in the mirror of its surface.

If water has this lovely facility of movement, then we should take advantage of it and use artificial means to increase the flow, getting a turbulence, a spray, a gurgle, a drip, a waterfall or a fountain! Modern equipment places at our fingertips all the inexpensive means of using water to best advantage.

An additional advantage of making the water move is that you improve its quality. It becomes aerated; pondweed, algae and other nuisances suffer inhibition in growth and fish enjoy the greater oxygenation.

To get water movement, you need a pump. This takes water from the pool and pushes it into the air from a fountain, up to the top of a waterfall or chute to tumble or cascade down any way you like. Pumps can be housed above the pool or submerged in it, depending on the functions they have to perform. Submerged pumps are small in size and consequently inexpensive, while surface pumps are sometimes quite large, powerful and more costly. Most of us, with a comparatively small pool, find we can manage with a small pump costing about £10 to £20 which produces a flow of several hundred gallons per hour.

Perhaps the most convenient of the small pumping systems is a submersible, virtually foolproof type. Completely silent in operation, it is joined to an electric supply, placed in the pool and operates immediately when the supply is switched on. It will operate a fountain or a waterfall and a built-in flow adjuster can be used to control the height of the fountain or the flow down the chute.

If, instead of a fountain, you prefer to move the water in a stream or waterfall, you will need plastic tubing to carry it from the pool to the source of the stream. This is generally the top of a bank, where a chute or series of chutes or streams leads down to the pool again. This plastic piping should, of course, be hidden both as it leaves the pool, by

This London town garden with its formal pool flanked by iris and other cool colour plantings would be an inviting place to sit on evenings following hot city days. It is also a garden which will demand little in the way of maintenance – a major consideration for those out at work all day and possibly away at weekends too

means of an overhanging rock or similar disguise, and as it winds to its exit. Here it can merely be buried a few inches under the soil.

Cascades and waterfalls are now as simple as garden pools to construct, for just as polythene liners and prefabricated plastic or fibreglass pools have done away with the necessity for concrete, so waterfalls, streams and cascades are now available, some with a natural rock finish that blends very happily into a rock garden. These can be used singly or in series, depending on the result desired and the space available.

Traditional pools with fountains and water cascades are not, however, to everyone's taste nor do they always fit harmoniously into some modern gardens. Fortunately, all water-flow systems are so flexible that the ways in which they can be used are almost limitless. To take a simple fountain, for example, there is no real reason why the jet should rise from the pool and fall into it again. The jet can be placed some distance away at an angle to allow the water to arc into the air before falling into the pool.

Again, there is no reason why the surface of the pool should consist of water. Some people prefer a pebble splash area. For this, the pool is constructed in the normal way but a platform of wire netting is stretched over the surface. On this is placed a layer of pebbles of different sizes, shapes and colours. The fountain jet rises through this layer from the filled pool beneath, and the falling spray of water keeps these pebbles permanently wet and glistening.

Once your pond is filled and you are sure it is clean you will need to furnish it with suitable plants of the aquatic type. The lovely water lily is probably the most popular. Nurserymen stock a wonderful range of these plants, which are not really lilies incidentally, but nymphaea and related to the lotus. But first just a word about aquatics generally. Almost all are perennials and as you would expect they may be hardy, half-hardy or tender. The latter are best for indoor aquaria or greenhouse pools. The first can be grown outdoors all the year through, though some disappear or almost so in winter; the second need to be protected from frost.

Most aquatic plants can be established from spring until early autumn. If you can, use rainwater rather than tap. In any case, allow the water to stand in the pool for a few days to become acclimatised before you plant. Half fill the pond so that the plants can be lowered in and then gradually fill the pond. Your choice of plants will depend upon the depth of water.

A pebble splash area can be a very attractive garden feature especially when sited on a patio

More ambitious water gardens are comparatively easy to construct with modern materials and electrical apparatus

Water plants are as varied as all other plants. You can have tall graceful ones, like the acorus or the variegated sweet flag, as well as the airy-fairy ones, such as the water saxifrage. You can have scented ones, such as preslia and you can have various colours. (And even if you don't want to go to the trouble of making a pond but would like some water plants, you can grow certain kinds in an old barrel cut in half and sunk in the ground or in a winecrock or sink.)

Aquatic plants are usually classified by the depth of water they need. Submerged aquatics with leaves that float on the surface usually need 12 to 18 inches over them. Others that need only their roots submerged will grow up out of the water. Some need only 3 to 5 inches or even just mud. And others are so easy that they will grow in any depth of water from 3 to 18 inches, their leaves and flowers standing above the water level. Others are merely tossed in and will float.

If you want to decorate the fringes of your water garden you will need marginal plants. There are two types catalogued. Some belong to the group of aquatics proper already mentioned. They need deep water from 6 to 18 inches and will grow from the bottom of the pool and rise well above the surface. The real marginal plants grow right on the edge, some with their toes just touching the water and others paddling in 4 inches of it. These are usually grown on a shelf round the pond, made especially for this purpose. If no shelf exists, they should be in shallow planting crates stood, to raise them, on bricks or stones.

The submerged oxygenating aquatics will give a depth and air of mystery to your pond as well as providing delightful places for fish to swim in and shade and protection for their young who, if they have no place of escape, get eaten by their elders. Most of these plants appear as no more than green shapes below the water, some, however, do flower.

There are floating aquatics, many of which are native plants, with delightful names such as fairy moss, water fan, floating water hyacinth, frogbit (a charming plant with small snow-white flowers very closely resembling water lilies), water lettuce, duck weed, crystalwort and water soldier (a curious plant with spiny foliage like a pineapple). This plant will lie submerged for a long time and then in the summer come to the surface to produce flowers; water chestnut is a rare and beautiful floating plant which has thin stems at the end of which there are large rosettes of deep green foliage and pure white flowers.

And when you have planted your pond and its margins, there are still many lovely perennials that can be grown by the waterside and which will give distinction to your garden. All they need is moist soil. Some will grow in semi-shade. They include several irises, the lovely day lilies, primulas, lythrum, and the tall showy lobelias.

Many people think that because so many of the pond plants need to grow from the bottom, the obvious thing to do is place a layer of soil on the base and plant them in this. This is quite good if you have an enormous pond, but hopeless for a little water garden. Once they are allowed to roam as they wish, the strong growing plants will dominate the others and you will have a bad job thinning them out. Instead, grow the submerged plants in pots, baskets or crates. If you have an old wicker basket no longer serviceable, you can use this to grow your water lilies in. In my own pond, I have used plastic planting crates and perforated pots. Wire-mesh containers can also be used. You have to make these yourself. Alternatively, if you make a concrete pond you can build planting pockets.

The soil for water plants must be very heavy. Well-rotted cow manure is most beneficial, so try to mix some with your soil, half and half. If you can't get cow manure, use a slow-acting fertiliser such as bonemeal. You will need roughly a tablespoonful to a bucketful of soil. Put this enriched soil in the lower half of the crate, ordinary soil above.

Water lilies thrive when they are planted in containers with openwork sides like this plastic planting crate. The soil should be very heavy and rich

If you make wire-netting crates yourself, line these with fibrous turf so that the loam does not escape. This is grass you have stripped off from parts of the garden and allowed to rot away, but not to disintegrate. Fill the crates with this, plant and lower them into the pond.

Water lilies come in many beautiful colours as well as white. One of the prettiest of the whites is delicately scented *Nymphaea odorata* which flowers from June to October. As well as white you can have rose-pink and salmon hues, deep wine, crimson and red; and copper, orange and yellow. There are certain miniature types which will grow in as little as 3 inches of water. But most water lilies require from 6 to 18 inches of water. If you want fish, then you need at least 18 inches of water in the deepest part of the pond. You must also take into consideration the depth of soil in which the lilies are planted and measure the depth of water above the soil surface. Water lilies must be in full sun. It is best to fill the pond slowly as the stems grow, so that the leaves are continually supported on the surface of the water. The alternative is to stand pots or crates on bricks, so that the first leaves float on the surface and to remove the bricks as the plants grow, but this is difficult I think.

Nuphars are other lovely aquatics whose under-water leaves look like translucent hart's tongue ferns but whose surface leaves look like water lily 'pads'. *N. lutea* is a pretty species for a pool. The lovely fragrant water hawthorn, aponogeton, will grow in a tub, pool or lake. In mild winters it will bloom until after Christmas! All these are for the centre of the pool.

The aim in every pool should be to have a good balance of plants and fish. Any supplier will advise on the number and types of plants and fish required for a specific pool. Without this proper balance, the water is certain to turn green and murky in the spring and early summer. Even with this balance, it is probable that a certain amount of algae will discolour the water in spring. This is nothing to worry about. The water will clear in a short while if it contains the correct balance of life.

When the pool becomes frozen over in winter, gases caused by decaying vegetation cannot escape easily, and if an accumulation of leaves lies at the bottom of the pool, harmful gases are given off in great quantities. Cold itself does little harm to fish, but lack of fresh air and toxic gases kill them. So keep part of the ice open on a frozen pond to maintain a supply of fresh air. Never break thick ice by banging it, for this causes something like an explosion which can kill fish. A rubber ball floating on the surface which you can move daily is one method of keeping an air-hole open.

People who have an electrically operated fountain or pump which is little used in winter could disconnect it and use the supply to operate an easily connected 100 watt pool heater instead. This should be switched on in severe weather only to keep a little area free from ice.

Rock gardens

A good rock garden is fascinating and rewarding. Alas, it's not easy to make. A pile of stones – often made as a means of getting rid of them – is no rock garden and is likely to be a perpetual disappointment. If you want a lovely rock garden you must be prepared to spend time and trouble.

Every rock garden must be constructed to suit its surroundings and its owner's taste. The aim, I think, is to provide such a natural effect that all the rock really seems to have become revealed by the weather denuding the soil from above it. To achieve this natural effect each rock must be very carefully placed with lines or strata on each piece running in the same and natural direction. It is, in fact, a labour of art and ingenuity.

Often, when for example you are excavating for a pond, a rock garden seems to follow naturally.

This rock feature separates one level of a garden from another and the bold use of colour will give constant pleasure during the spring. The old rock garden favourites of alyssum, aubrieta and iberis are complemented by the informal treatment of tulips and the daisy-flowered doronicums, one of the earliest of the perennials to flower

The soil can be thrown up to make a mound facing south east or south west – the ideal aspects for rock gardens – and also to give protection to the pond life from the north. A site facing due south can become too hot and dry, and one facing due north too cold. (However, it is possible to find plants that will suit these aspects, too.)

A rock garden should not be formal or of a precise shape. It should be placed in some spot where it will appear to merge happily with its surroundings. Although it should be sheltered (alpines are not necessarily happy in cold situations) it should not be dominated by trees or shrubs which may drip, or walls or fences which will cast heavy shade. Most rock garden plants are sun worshippers. You may have an area which is uneven, banked, or contoured in some way. Most rock gardens look prettiest on a slope and are often the answer to a garden problem, but you can also make them on a level site. If you are making a small garden, keep the shape simple. If it is to be fairly important, decide early on whether it is large enough for paths, stepping stones or steps.

Soil for a rock garden must be very good, for once made it will not be easy to refresh or replenish it. Drainage must be good but the soil must not be dry. Small stones will come in very useful for a rubble base which can be built up, then topped with soil. Finally, the good rocks can be placed to 'grow' from the good soil. This means that your plants will have an excellent start. The best soil is loam. If you know you are going to make a rock garden on some part of your lawn, remove the turves from the area and stack them in a neat pile grass-side downwards. They will soon rot and leave you with a heap of wonderful loam. No manure will be necessary. If you have no loam mix 3 parts soil, 1 part peat, leafmould or home-made compost and 1 part sharp sand.

The most expensive item is the rock itself. Local types of stone always look best. Obviously the nearer the source of stone the less money you will have to pay for transport. Limestone is a favourite. This is really beautiful and weathers well and attractively. Types include Westmorland, Derbyshire, Cotswold and Mendip. Sandstone, though soft and moist, becomes flaked by frost. (So does certain limestone, so be sure to take advice from your local dealer.) Quarried Westmorland sandstone is popular and good but it often looks 'new' for many years. Rock is heavier than one realises. A hundredweight of Westmorland limestone may sound a lot, but it could only measure about 18 inches by 12 by 6. Usually a ton of stone contains about 10 to 12

good pieces. Lightweight tufa stone is ideal and more easily handled than most other types.

A true rock garden gives the stone a chance to be seen and admired. Natural rock gardens, which one finds on mountains and hillsides, show only a little of the stone on the surface. This is the effect to aim for when placing the stones in position. Even if only a small area is below the soil there must be enough buried to anchor the rock securely. Most stones have a good face, so see that the most attractive side is placed outwards. When you 'seat' them, tilt the rocks backwards so that rain will be directed to the heart of the rock garden and the roots of the plants. Save stones you dig when clearing the garden to tilt, wedge and pack the rocks in place. Take care that no empty spaces are left at the back of the rocks or a plant may die of thirst. Little plateaux and pockets of soil made in front of a rock must always be in contact with the bulk of the soil. Remember that a flat stone is more likely to serve as a sun parlour for a plant than an upright one which often looks ill at ease.

Do not isolate the rock garden as though it were a little island in a sea of grass, but try to make it merge naturally with its surroundings as though it really and truly belonged. In some gardens extra rocks can rise to the surface a little distance away from the main rock garden. They can be fringed with grass and adorned with some lovely scrambler. A sharply defined cut edge between lawn and rock garden is ugly. Instead join it to the lawn level with a scree made of chippings or gravel. This also can form a path round the rock garden if you wish. Ground-hugging plants at the base of the rock garden will merge with the grass. If they are tough plants such as carpeting thyme, mowing the lawn will present no problem for these will not be harmed by the occasional shearing.

Alpines have different tastes and your soil is likely to grow some better than others. Some plants will grow best if peat or leafmould is worked into the place where they are to grow. Some like to be surrounded by limestone chippings. Others do not seem to mind at all, so long as they do not have to suffer heavy drips from trees.

Not only herbaceous perennials grow on rock gardens but there are also many delightful little bulbous plants which will flower in winter, spring or autumn. The range of naturally dwarf shrubs and trees is great and includes many enchanting plants. Many remain green all winter. When flowerless, the cushions, rosettes, carpets and drapes of lovely leaves are still decorative. Garden centres and nurseries everywhere stock many species and varieties, and all alpines are grown in pots and so can be transplanted at almost any time.

Incidentally, if it is the little alpine plants you want more than the actual rock garden, remember that many of these can be grown by other methods. You can, for example, grow them in a border made on what is known as a 'dry' stone wall. This is a double wall of stones set apart and the space between them filled with suitable soil. Plants are not only set in the wall-bound border but also between the stones of the wall. It is best if these can be planted as the wall is being built, so that you can ensure that their roots are firmly and well covered with soil. As plants have to be laid on their sides so that they grow over the surface of the wall, this is important. Walls of this kind can be as high as you wish and you may, in fact, find such a garden easier to maintain than a full scale rock garden. A wall up to $1\frac{1}{2}$ feet high need have no cement between the stones. Higher walls will need this strengthening at the base.

A similar wall to this may be very useful in dividing one portion of the garden from another. Also, if your garden is on a slope, a flat terraced area, supported by a wall of this type but single and not double, might look prettier. It is likely to be much easier to run.

A friend of mine grows many alpines in a sunny, well-drained bed which surrounds a formal pool. Here they seem to flower, one or other of them, the year through.

If pottering rather than active gardening suits your purpose, you might consider having an alpine house. This is an unheated greenhouse in which alpines are grown in flower pots or pans. Easy and cheap to run, it provides a place to work and to admire the plants no matter what the weather.

The fact that all the plants are growing on raised benches or staging means that bending is at a minimum – an important point for many who suffer from a bad back.

In all garden planning, building or re-making, it is wise to look to the future to consider the time when muscles will weary a little earlier and the back finds more difficulty in straightening up again after a bout of bending. One of the best ways to make gardening easier and quicker is to bring some of the work up to waist level.

When placing the stones in position for a rock garden the strata lines should all run in the same direction. Tilt the rocks slightly backwards and aim to give the impression that the majority of the rock is under the soil

The construction of a successful dry stone wall is quite a skilled operation but once completed it can give much pleasure and be very easy to maintain

Annuals, biennials, perennials

Annuals are those plants that have a brief, though often glorious, life. In one year they germinate from seed, grow, flower and produce seed themselves. Some take most of the four seasons to do this but others may complete this cycle more than once a year. Familiar examples of annuals are nasturtiums, Virginian stock, candytuft. (Some weeds also reproduce themselves several times in one year; groundsel is an example.)

A true annual never goes on growing in the second or third year, but some hardy annuals are tough enough to stand the winter either continuing in bloom – in mild winters until Christmas – or as seedlings when they flower the following year. Seed dropped in autumn from flowering plants will often lie dormant and germinate in spring. Mice and slugs take their toll of these and to ensure an early crop of hardy annuals many gardeners sow in spring.

In seed catalogues annuals are clearly divided into two groups, hardy and half-hardy. The latter are killed by frost and also need high temperatures before they will germinate. Usually most of the half-hardy annuals take so long to flower in our climate that they have to be given an early start indoors in an artificially induced spring or even summer temperature. Some seeds need a much higher temperature than others before they will germinate. For a heated greenhouse, a specially made propagator or some other warm place is necessary. On the seed packet containing half-hardy annuals you may read such advice as 'sow under glass'. This means in a glasshouse, not in a garden under a pane of glass. Often a sunny window-sill indoors provides a good nursery.

Half-hardy annuals should be planted out in the garden only when all danger of frost has passed. There are a number of plants which strictly speaking are half-hardy perennials, and which, in certain, though rare, circumstances will over-winter quite successfully. As most are killed by frosts, however, some half-hardy perennials are treated as half-hardy annuals; petunias are examples. These must be sown early enough in the spring to give them time to grow into plants mature enough to flower the same summer.

It seems to me that none of the popular annuals is very particular about soil (indeed some, such as nasturtiums, flower best in poor soil) though it should preferably be fairly well drained, sunny, well dug and broken up as finely as possible.

Seeds of hardy annuals can be sown at any time from March until May and some of the hardier types can even be sown in September. Examples of the latter seeds are: sweet peas, corn-flowers, candytuft, larkspur, calendula and annual chrysanthemum. Generally speaking, the earlier seed is sown the earlier it will germinate and flower. Seed sown in September will probably flower in June; seed sown in March and April will flower from July to September and seed sown in May will flower from August to October. It is possible, then, to extend the flowering time by saving some seed for later sowing. I always sow a few as late as June and early July, thus gambling on the autumn weather. It is surprising how often this pays off, and the bright spots of colour showing among the fallen leaves are doubly endearing. I use only the cheap packets of homely flowers for this.

In a seedsman's catalogue, you are likely to come across the terms, varieties, strains, hybrids, novelties, species. A species is a plant just as it occurs in nature, like the wild poppy. Every time it seeds the chances are that its seedlings will resemble the parent in every way. Very rarely a plant will vary from the specific type. The wild poppy did this once. The Rev. Wilks who lived at Shirley noticed that a wild poppy plant was a different colour from the rest. He collected seed from it, grew hundreds of seedlings, continually throwing away all the typical wild ones and saving only the ones that varied. These became known as Shirley poppies and they are a variety of the species.

Most seedsmen offer the same variety of a plant, but occasionally a seedsman will notice that a few of the plants are finer or more vigorous than the others. He will select these and breed only from them. These are called a good strain. Quite often the seedsman will give his name to a strain that he has selected in this way so that you might find something like Shirley poppy, Blank's Finest Mixed.

Hybrids are a cross between two species, just as the mule is the result of a cross between a horse and a donkey. If you save seed of a species, you will get plants which resemble their parents but seed you save of hybrids cannot be guaranteed to remain pure year after year.

Many of the novelties offered each year by seedsmen are varieties or hybrids or, more up to date, F_1 hybrids which mean that they are hybrids of a first generation cross. You cannot hope to save seed of these and see the same flower appear the following year. You are more likely to get an assortment of not so novel blooms. Usually novelties are dearer than those which are established.

You will see seed packets on sale almost anywhere and it is quite safe to buy them, for all seedsman have to conform to regulations laid down under the Seeds Act. They are liable at any time to have their seeds inspected and tested.

Seeds vary considerably in size and weight, not always in proportion to the size of the bloom. Snapdragons or antirrhinums for example, give some 220,000 seeds to the ounce, mignonette 30,000 and zinnia 28,000. So you can see that often a pinch of seed is enough for a small garden. Actually very few seeds are retailed by weight, most are measured.

If you want to grow large quantities of annuals for cutting or to cover quickly a large area (ideal for furnishing a new plot), you can buy many by the ounce or half ounce. This way they are very cheap. You can also buy mixtures, tall, dwarf, medium, suitable for children to grow or ideal mixtures to attract bees. I grow these mixtures myself and can recommend them.

Some seeds remain good for years but others quickly lose their vigour especially in a packet. One seedsman, at least, now markets some seeds in a new type of packet that ensures that they may be kept *unopened* for years.

People are apt to forget that seeds are alive. Rather than storing them in a warm, humid atmosphere, place them in the cool, dry environment of the garden shed or even the refrigerator. Stored in this fashion, the seeds will be longer lived.

If you have any seed of any plant left over from a previous year and you have doubts about its vigour, it is safest to sow it a little more thickly than usual or to sow a sample pinch indoors in a warm place so that it germinates quickly.

In nature, large and berry-like seeds for example often drop from the tree or bush on to soft mossy ground where they keep moist until the conditions are right for germination. If these are dried and packeted their vigour is lost and bad germination results. Many of these, like peonies, should be sown ripe. So must some herb seeds, especially those of the parsley family or *Umbelliferae*, yet parsley itself keeps its vigour for three years!

If you have berries from shrubs you would like to increase, half fill flower pots with sand, place the berries on this (they may be quite thick if you wish) and cover with more sand. Let this pot stay half buried in the soil in a cold place so that the berries will get frosted. This is called stratifying them. Sow them in the spring.

Many seeds and seedlings get lost in early life. Sometimes the finely raked soil in which they are sown attracts sparrows, who use it as a dust bath, see the seeds or seedlings and eat them, or alternatively take them away in their feathers.

Slugs are the great enemy of seedlings. Slug pellets should always be placed on the soil when seeds are sown. Frequently seeds are sown either too deeply or not covered sufficiently.

Hardy annual seeds are generally sown in the garden soil where the plants are required to bloom. Some of them, probably because of the taproots, do not transplant well and for this reason it is essential to sow seed thinly. Although there is no reason why the seed should not be sown in a straight row, except when they are grown for cutting only, it is generally more pleasing to sow in drifts or some less formal style. I use a flower pot pressed into the finely raked soil to make a circle. Seed can then be sown very thinly in this little drill. Twigs placed later in an outer circle help to support the young plants.

Always sow the seed very lightly, and cover with a fine sifting of soil or a little sand. Do not water unless the soil is dry. In really dry seasons, water the soil the day before. Germination will take from one to three weeks and as soon as the plants are large enough to be handled they should be thinned out. If plants are overcrowded they will be thin, drawn, unhealthy and unproductive. In general terms, it is suggested that small plants be thinned to about 4 inches apart, moderate-sized plants to about 8 inches and taller, larger varieties to 15 inches.

An easy way to create an informal effect with annuals is to sow the seed in a circular drill made by pressing a flower pot into finely raked soil

Annuals which were sown in the autumn should not be thinned until the following spring. On the other hand, if you are a keen flower arranger interested in miniatures, many unthinned annuals will give you delightful flowers on a small scale.

Half-hardy annuals can be treated in exactly the same way but sowing out of doors must be delayed until May. If you have a heated greenhouse, you can use this to get a start with seeds of some half-hardy varieties, sowing in boxes or pots of well-drained soil from February onwards. Use the easily obtained, standardised weed- and weed-seed-free John Innes Seed Compost, or one of the convenient, peat-based, no-soil mixtures. Seed should be scattered very thinly and covered lightly with sifted compost. Each box should have a pane of glass over it and this in turn should be covered with black polythene or other means of keeping out light. As soon as the seeds begin to germinate, the light should be allowed in and after the first two days' growth, the glass should be lifted slightly (a match stick on its side is enough) to allow slight ventilation. Two or three days later remove the glass entirely.

When the seedlings are large enough to handle, they should be removed to larger premises. The same type of compost can be used, but it is best to use John Innes Potting Compost No. 1. With a pointed wooden label, or special small dibber or similar instrument, lift each seedling carefully from its existing home, making sure not to damage roots in any way. Transfer to a pencil-sized hole made in the newly prepared box, pan or pot. Allow roughly 2 inches between each plant. Firm the soil around the young plant and water it well, using tepid water and a fine rose on the can.

As the plants continue to grow, they should gradually be hardened off by allowing them slightly more air and slightly cooler conditions. Finally the plants will be enjoying (or suffering) much the same conditions as any plants out of doors, and at this stage they can safely be planted out in the garden in their final positions. Use a trowel here, for the plants will be quite large, and make sure that the soil is well firmed around the roots. If there is any question of dryness in the soil, the plants should be watered in liberally. Remember that this is the tricky period. Up to now the young plants have been coddled and now they will be very much on their own, just at a time when they are about to fulfil their final function of being decorative in the garden. So a little care, particularly in watering, will be amply repaid.

Once the plants are away, growing well, showing their bloom and doing their part in making the garden pretty, one should ensure that they continue to do their duty for as long as possible. The primary function of a plant is to reproduce its species. It therefore tries to produce flowers and then seed. Once it begins to produce seed, it gives up producing flowers. So our move should be to prevent it producing seed. If we cut away all flowers that are fading, their seed cannot be produced and so the plant will continue to produce flowers in the hope that further seed may be forthcoming. This is the basic reason why dead or dying flowers should always be removed, so that more flowers will always come.

Biennials differ from annuals in that they take much longer to produce their blooms. In the garden, seed is usually sown in late spring for flowering the following spring or summer. True biennials flower one season and then die, but some do go on longer than one year and become perennial. Wallflowers which will continue for years are an example. As such long-lived biennials tend to become untidy, most gardeners prefer to make a fresh start.

In a small garden, it is wise to have them up and begin afresh, but biennials can help those with large gardens for they make good ground cover plants and usually look after themselves. In my own garden honesty grows well, its large leaves covering the soil from early summer on until the purple flowers come with the daffodils. I either allow the seeds to drop or I shake them from the silvery moons over areas I want them to colonise. I do the same with forget-me-nots (myosotis), sweet rocket, Sweet Williams and cheiranthus.

If you haven't raised biennials from seed yourself, it is almost always possible to buy plants in autumn from any garden centre. Some are also on sale in spring. It is safe to buy them if they are in flower; double daisies for example, are almost always sold in bloom.

Perennials are plants which live for many years but which die down or can be cut down in winter and which shoot again the following year. They are plants which do not, as a shrub does, form a persistent woody stem. Some perennials go on happily for year after year and for this reason they are very labour-saving. Some plants, Michaelmas daisies are an example, spread outwards, becoming bare in the centres. Because of this and to prevent spreading, plants in herbaceous borders are usually lifted regularly every few years, divided and replanted.

For perennial plants to live a long time and serve you well, they must have reasonably deep soil, which means that if your good topsoil is only shallow, then the subsoil a spit down must be forked over to aerate it well. Into it must be forked good, well-rotted manure, home-made compost, leafmould or, failing any of these, some peat to provide humus mixed with a long-lasting fertiliser such as bonemeal or a good general organic fertiliser, and the plants should be mulched with compost or dung in late autumn or winter.

Many perennials can be raised from seed, and if these are sown early in the year the plants may flower later the same year; delphiniums and lupins are examples. Most of them, however, do not flower until the following year.

It is possible to find perennials that will flower from very early in the year until late autumn. Many of them are noteworthy for their beautiful, distinctive and handsome foliage which is often much more striking than their blooms.

The traditional herbaceous border, placed for protection against a warm wall, fence or hedge, has been for many years the only accepted way of growing a display of these plants. But such borders have their limitations, since they are not always as showy as people like for much of the year. Because of this mixed borders consisting of small trees, shrubs and all kinds of other herbaceous plants are taking their place – and very successfully too!

Another drawback to the traditional border is that it needs staking and continual maintenance. There are many perennials which need no staking and more are being continuously introduced. To be seen at their glorious best the taller and more sappy of perennials need shelter from the wind but the tougher types can be grown in island beds which fit prettily into informal garden schemes. This also is a good method to use if you have no protective backing such as a wall or fence. In an island bed, the plants should be grouped so that one can look through the bed from some point to the other side. There are many ground covering and dwarf growing plants for the edges and a selection of plants rising to the taller kinds in the centre or to one side, according to the plans of the rest of the garden, will give depth as well as expanse of colour.

The stakes of taller plants are bound to show in the early stages, but before you decide on the method of support, visualise the plant in its flowering stage and arrange to have the top of the stakes just hidden by the top flowers and leaves. Too short a support sometimes causes the stems to bend over at the point where the stake ends, so beware!

For plants that have several stems rising from ground level or for those that begin branching fairly near the ground, the best supports are pea sticks, the twiggy kind. Push these round the plant, only 2 or 3 inches away from it, letting the twigs intermingle. The plant's stems will grow up between them and be supported by them. They will in time hide the twigs completely. Cut the twigs to the correct height for the plant. Use short top pieces for dwarfer plants.

For tall and large flowering dahlias you need a really strong support. Garden stores sell special dahlia stakes which should be driven deep into the ground. Alternatively, use three stout bamboos grouped round the plant. Use strong twine to confine the plant within them or tie each stem to a single stake.

You may need to make a higher tie later in the season. Never pull the string so tight round the plants that it makes a kink in the stems. Give them room to breathe and expand.

A so-called perennial border can be supplemented by more tender plants such as dahlias which must be lifted and their tubers stored in a frost-proof place in winter, after which they may be planted in following years. Careful planning is needed. Quite often in such borders, and even in catalogues listing perennials, are included plants which strictly are shrubs. These include lavender, ceratostigma, thymes. They are doubly pleasant because they help to clothe the border prettily when it is not in flower, since they are also evergreen.

Bulbs, corms and tubers are also perennials and those that do not need lifting too frequently and which are large enough may also be included in the border. These include montbretias, *Hyacinthus candicans* and lilies as well as the spring-blooming kinds.

The smaller and the narrower your border, the shorter will be the season because your selection will be restricted. Ideally you need a border about 5 feet wide for then you will have enough room to allow plants coming into season to hide those just fading. If you begin with certain spring plants, such as lovely lupins, you can follow these with stately delphiniums, peonies and so on to the full range of phloxes and other summer flowers and on into the Michaelmas daisies, golden rod and hardy chrysanthemums of autumn.

Mixed borders which contain plantings of perennials, shrubs, flowering bulbs and annuals are very popular features especially in smaller gardens. With careful planning they can provide year-round colour and interest with maintenance reduced to a minimum.

53

Sowing seed and transplanting

If you have ever sown seed across an open plot and seen it all disappear from the depredations of pests, birds, frosts or droughts, the advantages of a special nursery bed where the soil is fine and easily tended and the seedlings fairly close together for inspection will be obvious to you. You will find that a raised bed is better drained and warmer than flat soil because it has a greater surface to catch the sun's heat. Make it roughly the same shape as an upturned roasting tin. Site it in a place which gets a little shade but which is not actually shady all day. Its size depends upon your garden but it needs to be at least a yard square or more.

I have my own nursery bed inside the cage which covers my vegetable garden. You will find that you can protect your seedlings from birds (or from cats) by taking a piece of small-mesh wire-netting and folding it down the centre to make a tent. Either make it longer than you need and fold the ends over to close them or cut two triangles to fit. You can fix them in position by pushing bamboos through them and so peg them into the ground or, alternatively, you can hook the wire ends round each other. I use clothes pegs to secure them. If you wish to cover this tent with polythene for the purpose of keeping frost out, this can also be secured by using pegs.

Find some good soil for your seedbed. I always take the precaution of putting a layer of John Innes Seed Compost on the surface and I find this worthwhile, for it does seem to give the plants a better start, and the weeds are kept at a minimum. It should be so fine and of such a good texture that you can draw drills very easily. You will not need a real line

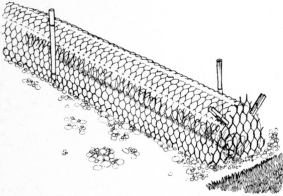

A tent made from small-mesh wire-netting can be erected over seedlings to protect them from birds and household pets. This serves a dual purpose for it can be used to support polythene to keep frost out in severe weather

but you will need a guide. You can use your rake handle or a cane. If you have made a large bed, use a plank to walk on as you make the rows but remember that two or three small beds are easier to manage than one large one.

Put down slug pellets if you find these pests a nuisance. Place them under a stone if you have pets. Stretch cotton over the bed if you are troubled by dust-bathing sparrows or alternatively, lay fine twigs over the soil surface. These will also, like the wire-netting I mentioned earlier, give shade.

Use this seedbed for biennials, perennials and some vegetable plants such as brassicas, leeks and lettuce.

Generally speaking, a large seed needs to be buried twice its own depth. Small seed should be just covered to prevent it blowing away.

Vegetable seeds and flowers specially grown for cutting are sown in drills. For these the ground must first be dug – in the autumn if possible. If you are sowing seed in borders among other plants, use a small border fork. If it is not advisable to dig deeper than an inch or two, then merely scratch the surface to take the seed and import soil to cover it. Alternatively, you can use fine silver sand to cover the seed. This will also provide a marker and remind you where the seeds are sown.

Soil surfaces must be dry for seed sowing although the soil must be moist below. If your shoes stick to the soil it is too wet for seed. On large areas first rake the soil level walking backwards as you do, so covering foot marks and bringing with you all old roots, bits of stick and large stones.

Incidentally, if you mark the handle of your rake in feet and six-inch lengths you have a handy measure.

To make a drill, use a draw hoe, one with a crook neck. Hold the handle, stand at one end of the line, tilt the hoe letting its back run along the line and draw a furrow or a drill through the soil. Avoid making this drill too deep for tiny seeds, but remember that the furrow is deceptive and is twice as deep as the drill, because of the ridge of soil on each side. But if seeds are not sown deep enough, they are liable to be raked to the surface later. Sow small seeds from the packet mixing them with sand if they are very small. Large seeds should be poured into a dish and then scattered by hand.

Always mark each end of a drill with a cane or stick before removing the line after sowing. Take the rake and, using the *back*, gently pull it along one side of the drill to cover the seed. Treat the other side the same way to level the soil again. Walk down the row pressing the soil lightly with your (low heeled) shoes. But do not leave it tramped hard like this. Just scratching the surface (if you go too deep you will bring the seeds to the surface) walk backwards and rake the soil, herring-bone fashion, until it looks groomed again. Do not walk on it again until the seeds show through. Place a label against one of the sticks. Make the drill for the next row using the sticks at each end of the row as markers.

The difference between a plant that has been given plenty of room and one which has to fight for its existence is really remarkable, so if you have sown seeds of annuals do not let them remain crowded. You must thin them out as soon as they are 1 inch high or large enough to be handled. Although there are exceptions usually the seedlings can be planted somewhere else, so need not be wasted.

Wait for a shower so that the soil is moist before lifting the seedlings. Roots are covered with fine hairs which cling to the soil particles through which the plant takes its soluble food from the soil, so disturb the roots as little as possible. The more soil you take with the plant the fewer hairs are broken and the less damage you do and so give less shock to the plant. The smaller the shock the quicker will the plant get away in its new home. One reason why it is good to mix peat in the soil is that the root hairs cling well to it.

First thin out so that the plants clustered in a group are all about 3 inches apart every way. If you thin more than this at first and a plant gets eaten or damaged you will have to fill in instead of thinning out! Remove more plants when they begin to touch each other.

For very small seedlings an old kitchen fork will raise them out with little damage. Don't let those you want to move lie in the sun but make the interval they are out of the soil as short as possible. If you want to give them or take them away slip them in a plastic bag, and close the end.

If you want merely to thin out, not to transplant them, either cut very crowded ones out with a pair of scissors or pull them out between finger and thumb.

Taking cuttings, making layers and dividing

As you may know, many plants can be raised from cuttings, the name given to portions of plants such as stem, leaf or root which will root when detached from the plant and placed in a suitable material. We talk of striking cuttings. Not all are easy to root, but since so little time and money are involved they are well worth trying.

Leaf cuttings are mainly taken from house and greenhouse plants. Some will root merely by being placed in water, others by being pressed into a box or pan of sandy soil or a half peat, half sand mixture. So long as the underside of the leaf lies flat on the rooting medium it should root. Some large leaves, ones like the *Begonia rex,* are often secured by hairpin-like wires passed over the main veins. The leaf becomes more readily rooted if these veins are slit quite drastically every inch or so, which results in a very ragged leaf indeed. Roots appear at these cuts and little tufts of leaves (crowns) often appear too, so that from one leaf more than one plant can be raised.

The propagation of *Begonia rex* by leaf cuttings

55

Leaf cuttings need a warm, and if possible, moist atmosphere. Bottom heat is often recommended. Gardeners without a greenhouse can provide this if the cuttings are stood on a shelf over a radiator so long as the box or pan is enveloped in a transparent plastic bag to keep the compost damp and the atmosphere around the leaf cuttings moist. Not all leaves will root.

Certain plants can be grown from root cuttings. Best known are anchusa, hollyhock (a good way of propagating a particularly good-coloured variety) gaillardia, phlox, oriental poppy, perennial statice and verbascum. Some roots will be very much thicker than others but this seems to have no bearing on the ease with which they can be propagated.

In winter, portions of the root, $1\frac{1}{2}$ to 2 inches long, should be placed either upright or on their sides in the rooting medium, just below the surface. Since most of the plants are hardy, the cuttings may then be kept in a cold frame or in an unheated greenhouse. They should be ready as little plants for transplanting by the next summer.

The most popular type of cuttings are stem cuttings. These are divided into soft-wood, half-ripe or hard-wood sometimes called 'naked' cuttings. Most soft cuttings are taken at the nodes or joints. Obviously the length of a cutting will depend upon the type of the plant, but the general rule is to find a shoot with three or four joints, not counting the growing tip.

Soft types of cuttings lose moisture easily and quickly. They can be helped if you can keep the air round them moist. Some will root uncovered in a pot, box or frame but it often helps if they are placed under a cloche or in a polythene tent. An easy and efficient way is to take a transparent polythene bag and slip the filled pot inside it. It should then be inflated and secured so that it is virtually airtight. There will be condensation and so long as this appears as a light mist over the inner surface of the bag, all is well. If, however, you have made the rooting medium too wet, the condensation may be so heavy that it will cause the cuttings to rot or to damp off. The best thing to do in this case is to remove the bag, turn it inside out and slip it back on again and secure as before.

A propagating frame or box is sometimes used. This is placed on the staging of a greenhouse or on a warm window-sill. This is a small box with a closed transparent lid. The box is half filled with peat or other similar material which is moistened and the boxes and pans are stood on this. If bottom heat is added, roots form very quickly but guard

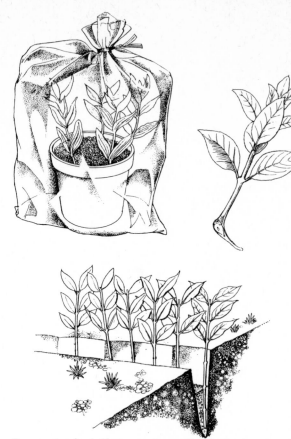

Propagation by half-ripe cuttings with a heel (above) and hard-wood cuttings

against creating too much moist heat or fungus will attack the cuttings. Probably the ultimate in luxury and certainly of success is provided with a mist propagation unit, which keeps cuttings moist and results in rapid rooting.

Soft cuttings root very easily in sand, which may be used instead of a cutting soil mixture, but when this is so the cuttings must be transferred very quickly from sand to soil once they have rooted, or they will become starved. If you can get them growing quickly after rooting you get a much better plant.

Although cuttings may be given individual pots, one popular method is to insert several cuttings round the rim of a clay pot in such a way that they actually touch the cool inner surface. This not only saves space and time but appears to be beneficial, because cuttings really do root quicker when struck this way. At least one third the length of the stem of a cutting needs to be inserted in the rooting medium. No leaves must be allowed to remain on the portion to be inserted, so trim them off with a sharp knife or scissors. Roots form round the underground joints where the leaves once grew.

Many shrubs, including heathers, are propagated by taking half-ripe cuttings, those shoots which have not yet become really woody but are, all the same, nearly matured. They are usually taken in midsummer, June, July and early August. These are often, like the soft cuttings, taken at a joint or node, and so are known as 'nodal' but many more are 'heeled'. These cuttings are sideshoots which are not cut or nipped from a plant as they would be for soft-wood cuttings. Instead, they are pulled downwards in such a way that a heel of the tissue of the main stem comes with them. (It is known that the cells in this area initiate roots quickly.) The heel needs trimming, though, to remove the very end which might decay. The lower leaves on the shoot should also be removed.

It is possible to divide a long (over 6 or 7 inches) heeled shoot into two. The tip heel-less portion should be cut just under a leaf joint or node. Remove its lower leaves. Heels are not essential but heeled cuttings will usually be found to root more quickly.

You do not need to take quite so much trouble over half-ripe cuttings as you do over soft-wood cuttings because they do not lose so much moisture. A frame or a propagating frame in a greenhouse is most generally used so that the atmosphere will still be warm and humid but not excessively so.

Less trouble still are the hard-wood or naked cuttings. As one might expect, little moisture is lost by these; they do not need a special climate and may be rooted outdoors. Many currants and other hardy shrubs will stand the winter without any protection but evergreens are generally inclined to be a little more tender and these are best taken in a cold frame, or under a cloche. This does not mean to say that the light (the cover) of the frame must be left on all the time. It is needed in severe weather only. It is important that these cuttings be well-ventilated. Some people use a frame cover made of thin laths of wood.

Hard-wood cuttings are taken in October or November, at the end of the growing season when the wood is ripe. This means that they are necessarily divided into deciduous and evergreens. All of them are likely to be much larger than the other types previously discussed. Evergreens must be stripped of the lower leaves.

To contain the hardy cuttings, make a trench in the open ground but choose a spot as sheltered as possible. The trench is easily made by inserting a spade for a little way into the soil and levering it forward to make a V-shaped slit. Line the bottom of the trench generously with coarse sand. This will promote root growth and it will also help to keep the trench well drained. Place the cuttings along the back of the trench, 2 or 3 inches apart and from 2 to 4 inches deep, making sure that the bases of the cuttings are really in contact with the sand. Replace the soil round the cuttings, then press each one in firmly by treading round it.

Most cuttings wilt a little, but this is nothing to worry about. The very fact that they flag a bit means they will begin to push out roots in search of water. When they perk up, you can be pretty certain that they are rooting.

The quicker the roots are formed the better. It is possible to buy certain hormone rooting powders or liquids to speed up this process. Some cuttings are just dipped in the powder before being struck, sometimes the powder is mixed with the soil. Other times the cuttings are stood in a solution for 24 hours or longer. Usually 'hard' cuttings, those taken from woody shrubs or plants, need longer preparation. You will find directions on the packet or bottle.

The speed with which roots are formed varies according to the type of cutting. If all conditions suit them, the soft types should root in three or four weeks. Half-ripe cuttings taken in the summer should be ready for transplanting into pots or nursery beds by the autumn. Hard-wood types are slow to root, often not starting until the spring, and will not be ready for transplanting until about a year after they were taken.

I often strike cuttings in rows in a bed in a frame, for I find this less work than filling pots with cutting sand or soil. I have found it best first to spread a layer of ashes, for this appears to discourage slugs as well as to ensure good drainage, then on this to spread a 3-inch layer of the cutting compost and then finally a thin layer of silver sand. If only a few cuttings are to be taken, just a section of the bed in the frame is prepared in this way. The cuttings should then be dibbled in, spaced about an inch apart all ways. As the dibber is inserted and removed, and the cutting put in its place, some sand will trickle in – a good thing for this aids rooting. The soil must be pressed firmly round the cuttings.

If you have no frame, you can convert a bottomless box to hold cuttings. A pane of glass or clear plastic should be placed on the top when soft cuttings are taken. It is a wise precaution to stand pots containing cuttings on ashes.

You can also make a good temporary frame by using the warm wall of your house, so long as this will not look too unsightly! Do not choose a spot where the mid-day sun strikes fully, for frames need partial shade. Make a wooden frame to the size that will be practical. Fill up with peat and top with a layer of sand or soil and sand and cover with polythene. If you have an old window frame for the 'light' or cover, so much the better. If you want to do the job really well, you can install an electric soil-heating unit.

If you grow garden blackberries or rambler roses you may have noticed that, where a long shoot has bowed over and touched the soil, new roots have formed and have probably even grown into the ground. In fact, the plant has layered itself and is on the way to producing a daughter plant. If you sever the rooted stem from its parent, you can move it elsewhere to grow as an independent plant. We call such a plant a layer and use this technique, 'tip-layering' to grow more plants.

A branch of most shrubs, including rhododendrons, will throw out roots down its stem if this is allowed to come in contact with the soil. The roots will grow quicker if the bark of the stem has become damaged. Often this happens by accident but we can *make* it happen too. This also is called layering and it is the easiest way to increase or propagate shrubs. Choose a low-lying branch and select a good vigorous one.

Bend it down and note at what point it touches the soil. At this point make a cut on the underside, so that a little tongue of bark and tissue is formed. This cut must then be set below soil level. Scoop out a little depression and, in this, peg the branch to the soil. It helps if you can place a little prepared rooting compost in the depression. Mix some sharp sand and a little peat with good soil to make the compost, and let a little of this compost cover the branch.

To ensure that the branch stays where it is, and to keep the soil moist and to act as a marker to remind you where the layer is, cover the soil with a large stone. It will be some months before the layer has rooted enough for you to cut it away from its parent plant and transplant it elsewhere, but you will be able to judge when it is ready by the pull of the roots when you test it. Some people prefer to fill a flower pot with good soil, to plunge it up to its rim in the ground and to root the layer in this.

You can also layer carnations. These plants consist of a group of tufted growths, some of which have flowered, some not. For layers, choose non-flowering growths. Bend them away from the plant and

Layering is an easy means of increasing rhododendrons, azaleas and other shrubs. Tie the end of each shoot to a cane so that it is held in an upright position

note which part of the bare stem touches the soil. Here the stem must be cut or nicked to interrupt the sap flowing along it. The plant will then seek other means – new roots in this case – to support itself.

To make the incision, cut a little slice in the under portion of the stem. Begin by taking the knife through a joint where the bud lies hidden, and up towards the tip of the shoot, but only for a little way to the base of the next joint. You can now see why this method of layering is called tongueing or heeling, for a loose tongue of stem is formed.

So that it stays in contact with the soil, peg down the shoot. You can use a bent wire or a cleft stick for this. The shoot must be covered with soil so that the cleft stem is buried and you must take care that the cut surfaces are kept open as the soil covers them. So that you have a neat erect plant, stake the end of the shoot so that it grows upright.

You can take any number of layers from one plant, so long as you choose branches or shoots that have not flowered. It is often best to spread the layers out, making a ring round the centre of the plant. Keep the soil moist and the roots should be formed in a few weeks. Sever the layer from the parent plant in September and plant elsewhere, any time from two weeks after you have severed it.

For pinks or dianthus, the special type of cutting which we call a piping takes best. You will find

Taking a carnation piping

the pipings growing quite abundantly round the base of old plants, each being a perfect little individual shoot that has not bloomed. They must be taken from the plant soon after it has finished flowering.

Hold the piping in your right hand and pull it from the parent plant. You will find the stem will be pulled out from a low pair of leaves rather as you pull the hull from a strawberry. It is this soft pull-out piece of stem which will give rise to the roots. But first of all you must remove a few of the lower leaves. Don't just strip these down the stem in case you injure the tiny bud which forms in the axil of every true leaf and its stem. Instead, take a knife or a pair of scissors and carefully snip off the leaf, leaving just the smallest fraction of the base near the stem.

Some people like to trim the base of the piping by making a new cut just below the lowest joint with a sharp knife.

Now you must strike the pipings, and this is best done under cover in the same way as described for cuttings. Insert the pipings about an inch apart each way. You can mix varieties if you wish. You should keep the glass shaded from very bright sunlight; a piece of brown paper placed over it on very hot days will do, or even two leafy boughs set over the glass tent-wise.

Many new plants can be obtained by dividing existing ones. Generally speaking, you can divide them between September and March. If they flower late, then division must wait and follow flowering, not precede it. Not even nurserymen agree about the best season to divide plants. Some, for example, send out Michaelmas daisies in October, others in March.

Another general rule is that one plants fibrous-rooted plants in autumn, sappy-rooted plants in the spring. There is one drawback to this rule – beginners surely are not likely to know what plants have which kinds of roots – but still it is a tip worth remembering.

Old perennial plants are inclined to go bald in their centres. They should be divided so that the good outside pieces are retained. One rule that always irritates me is that gardeners are told to take two digging forks, place them back to back in the centre of a large root and then pull them apart, dividing the plant. This is all right but I wonder how many gardeners have two digging forks? Often I cut my plants in chunks with one good spade chop! Others can be pulled apart with the aid of a fork.

Perennial plants that will live for years giving lovely flowers or foliage need not be lifted unless they obviously are becoming old in the centre. Most are best if lifted every three years. Some, like peonies, dislike being moved around at all and may not flower the year after moving. You can choose a good piece of the plant to put back in the original site and cut or break the others into nice-sized clumps to grow elsewhere. If you have no room in the border, you might consider planting a few rows across the garden somewhere so that you can always have plenty of flowers to pick. If you want to get a lot of plants you can divide a clump into really small pieces so long as each piece has a good root.

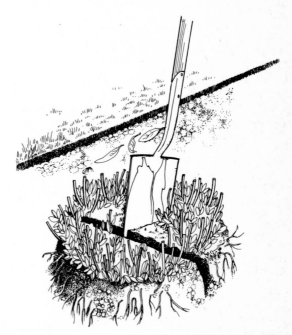

Most herbaceous perennials will benefit if they are lifted from the border every three years or so and divided into smaller portions. The older centre can then be discarded

Let science help in the garden

Soil husbandry is the oldest of the arts, and one of the newest of the sciences. Basically we grow our plants in very much the same way as has been done for thousands of years. Yet we prepare and cook the fruit and vegetables we grow using the latest methods, appliances and aids.

The reason behind this is mainly one of economics. We are prepared to spend a certain amount of money on a modern kitchen but the sums necessary to install every latest scientific help in the garden are out of all proportion to the probable increase in crop and decrease in time and labour involved.

A lawnmower, obviously, is a necessity for all but the tiniest of lawns. But a motor-driven machine is normally wasted if an able bodied person has to cut an area of less than about 1,500 square feet. A small hand-powered machine will cost about one-tenth of the price and carry out the task just as quickly and efficiently.

Mowers are of two types. The more conventional kind makes use of a revolving cylinder which is geared to the wheels or a roller. When the wheels revolve, powered either by machine or by pushing, the cylinder revolves and cuts the grass against a base plate, much like a pair of scissors. Some motor-driven mowers have a cut-out device so that the engine can be disconnected and this is helpful when it is desired to control the machine (as with a tricky corner) more carefully than is possible when it is being pulled forward by the engine.

The second type of machine is available in powered form only, and the cutting blades are either mounted on a flat plate or can take the form of two or more knife blades which revolve at speed parallel to the ground. This type slashes or scythes the grass rather than cuts it. Some, but not all of this type have collecting boxes or sacks into which the mown grass is blown. In general this type is particularly suited to long and rough grass which cannot satisfactorily be cut by a cylinder mower. Some, however, give a remarkably fine finish, and those with a rear cylinder instead of wheels will even leave the striped effect up and down the lawn left by the best cylinder mowers.

If your garden is large and you wish to mechanise most of the tasks in which it involves you, it is possible to buy multi-purpose machines with attachments that will cultivate your soil, trim your hedges, saw your timber, prune your trees, carry your loads, spray, pump, and carry out many other tasks. After all, you can only do one job at a time, so you only need one source of power, and this can be harnessed to assist you in each of these many tasks.

Powered machines today need not be petrol driven. They can be run by electricity, either from the mains or from portable batteries. The advantages of mains electricity are that it is more or less foolproof, starts with the flick of a switch and it is blessedly quiet. On the other hand it necessitates a long cable from the house or other access point. It can be dangerous if cables are frayed or otherwise damaged or if the machine is handled carelessly. To obviate this, many machines can be adapted to run on a safe low voltage, supplied from the mains source but via a step-down transformer and today all machines are double insulated for the greatest possible degree of safety.

It is sometimes more convenient to use batteries. These can be very heavy, but mounted on a well-balanced machine they are little heavier than a petrol-driven motor. Battery-driven machines are again quiet and almost as foolproof as mains electricity so long as the batteries are kept charged and in good condition. Most battery-driven machines are supplied with a charger, so that at the end of a working session they require only to be plugged in to a mains point overnight to be ready for work again next morning. The batteries generally carry a charge that will enable them to be used for up to two hours, which means that if you have more than half an acre or so of lawns to mow, the batteries may not last you the whole of the time. Garden machinery suppliers will always advise.

A number of small hand tools such as hedge trimmers are now available with integral, lightweight batteries which can be readily recharged. This does away with awkward cables, and makes them safer to handle.

Of the attachments available for a machine, unquestionably the most useful is the digging equipment. This can consist of revolving cultivator blades which can dig and pulverise the soil to a depth of up to a foot or so depending on the model, or plough blades which will turn over the soil but not necessarily break it up. Only comparatively large areas of land, frequently cultivated, make these attachments economic.

It is possible in many parts of the country to hire machines of various types by the hour or by the day and this is a useful service when a once-only job is to

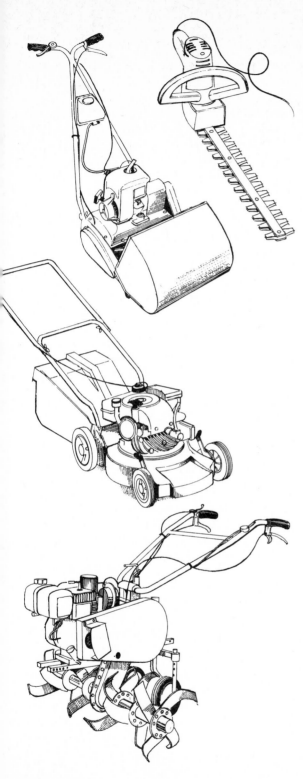

A selection of the many powered tools now available for the busy gardener. From top to bottom these are a hedge trimmer, cylinder mower, rotary mower, and cultivator

be tackled, such as the ploughing of a considerable virgin area. Alternatively, more and more garden contractors are appearing on the scene parallel with the disappearance of the jobbing gardener.

But machines are not the only aid that science has given us in the past decade. Chemicals can also help us. There has been some outcry against garden and farm chemicals and it is true that mistakes have been made with them, but used intelligently some of them can be of the greatest value to the gardener and can do no possible harm. In general they can be divided into three types: weedkillers, insecticides and fungicides. In addition there are chemical fertilisers.

Unfortunately, under these labels there exists such a proliferation of types and names, some proprietary and some chemical, that the average gardener is both confused and tempted to buy far more than he needs.

Most gardeners with what is known as ordinary soil need have in their armoury no more than one fertiliser, three types of weedkiller, one insecticide and one fungicide. It may also be helpful to have a small supply of garden lime and a certain quantity of granulated peat.

The fertiliser can be of almost any type, liquid, powder or granular. If the general principles of good gardening are followed, then the soil should be in good condition and rich enough to grow most crops well. Fertilisers should be used only to give a boost or spurt to crops, floral, arboreal or vegetable, at the beginning of spring, so that they give of their best for the remainder of the year.

There are three basic chemicals necessary to healthy plant life. These are nitrogen, phosphorus (phosphoric acid) and potash. The chemical symbols for these chemicals are respectively N, P and K. Nitrogen promotes lush leaf growth, phosphorus helps the production of strong roots and potash gives ripening and fruit production. It is possible to obtain fertilisers which contain different proportions of these chemicals, but in general most so called 'balanced' fertilisers which you buy in garden stores contain NPK in proportions that will bring well-balanced growth to the plant in all ways. Legally, all commercial fertilisers must carry information about their NPK content, usually abbreviated into percentages such as 5:3:2. All proprietary fertilisers have their virtues and so long as they are used with discretion and strictly according to maker's instructions they can do no real harm.

Weedkillers can also be a help to the gardener. There are three main types: total weedkillers that will kill all plant life for long periods; selective weedkillers used to kill broad-leaved weeds in grass, leaving the grass unharmed; and the latest type, a total weedkiller which has no residual effect on the soil.

Total weedkillers which have a long life should be used only on paths and other areas where plants are not to grow. If they are used to clear an area which will later be planted, then a period of several months must elapse between application and planting so that it can be leached from the soil. Some of these weedkillers tend to creep in the soil so must not be used too close to trees, lawns or borders or these are likely to be affected. Others are obtainable which will not creep, and one of these, a simazine-based weedkiller, is particularly long lasting and will keep a path or drive clear of all weeds for a year or more. But it also means that the sprayed area will be totally unsuitable for planting of any type for an even longer period.

Selective weedkillers are particularly helpful for lawn culture, for they do not harm grass if applied at the correct rate yet they keep down the weeds which grow in the grass. Two or three applications a year should keep any average lawn free from weeds.

The third type of weedkiller has been described as a chemical hoe, for it is designed to act in much the same way. It acts on the green part of a plant only and when it touches the soil it is completely inactivated. So if there are weeds growing in the rose bed or the vegetable garden they can be sprayed with this paraquat-based weedkiller and the weeds wetted will die in a matter of a day or two; no green part of the rose bushes or the vegetables must be touched by the liquid. Brown tree or bush stems will not be affected and soil will not be contaminated. It is thus possible to spray a weedy area one day and a day or two later plant in the same spot.

All of these weedkillers are applied in liquid form with one exception. The exception is a selective weedkiller known as lawn sand used on lawns for killing broad-leaved plants. It is generally marketed in conjunction with a lawn fertiliser so that weeds are killed and the lawn fed in a single operation. This powdered or granular form of selective weedkiller can be spread by hand or by a special spreading machine which is merely pushed over the lawn and allows regulated portions to fall on to the grass.

Liquid weedkillers are usually diluted with water and sprayed by means of a watering-can. Instead of the usual watering-can rose, special spray bars are available which spread the spray to cover wider areas, or to confine the spray to certain well-controlled areas. It is wise always to keep a special watering-can for weedkillers and to mark this clearly.

Nearly all insect pests in the garden are either suckers or chewers; they suck sap from the leaves or chew them. Among the former type are aphids such as greenfly and blackfly and among the latter are caterpillars. It is not sufficient then, if we wish to rid ourselves of both types with one spray, merely to spread a poison on the leaf surface, for the sap is not affected. There are several types of systemic insecticide available to us which will kill most kinds of insects. These not only spread a poison on leaf surfaces; they are actually absorbed into the system of the plant so that the sap contained is also contaminated.

I cannot too strongly emphasise that an insecticide of this type is lethal and it must therefore be used with the utmost care and as seldom as possible. Never allow it on your hands and do not let any spray blow into your face or on to your clothes. If your skin is contaminated wash at once. Never allow these insecticides near children, never spray open flowers during the day or beneficial insects will also be killed. Spray only when you are sure that pests are present. Read the label on the bottle, can or packet with great care and follow instructions implicitly.

Fungicides, on the other hand, are more successful when used as a preventive rather than a cure. They are much less effective, for example, in curing black spot and mildew on roses than in preventing these diseases. And as they are not toxic to birds and animals in the same way as an insecticide they can be applied before the disease becomes apparent and applied in regular doses to prevent the disease from appearing and spreading. Some fungicides are now systemic, and work in a similar way to the systemic insecticides.

These, then, are the basic chemical aids in killing or preventing insect and disease attack. Occasional war must be waged against other pests such as slugs, ants and wasps, but clean and thorough gardening can help keep all these pests and diseases to a minimum.

Good gardening obviously depends mainly on the soil and although soil improvement has been discussed at the beginning of this book I have not gone into detail about special soils. I have mentioned garden compost and John Innes soil mixtures but have not said how they should be made.

Garden compost is composed of rotted vegetable matter. The best available natural soil is leafmould and this is composed of leaves, twigs and other vegetable matter that has naturally fallen to the

of inches of soil. Layers of this sort should be continued until the heap reaches the top. In practice it will seldom be found that the top is reached, for the material will rot quite quickly and settle downwards. Special compost accelerators can be bought which will speed the rotting process, but these are not essential and even without them it will be found that roughly two loads of compost a year can be removed and used on the garden.

The heap should not be allowed to get too dry and in periods of drought it will be helpful to give it a good watering occasionally. On the other hand it must not be allowed to get waterlogged, so in bad weather it is helpful to cover it with perhaps a large sheet of polythene weighted down by stones.

It will be found that the centre of the heap usually rots down into good soil more quickly than the outside, so it helps to turn the outside to the centre and vice versa when it is apparent that this is necessary.

Garden compost is both a fertiliser and a provider of much needed humus, so the more that can be made the better for your garden soil. Use it lavishly as a mulch, alternatively, dig it into the top few inches of soil and keep the compost heap always going to provide a continuity of supply.

Mention has been made in certain sections of this book of John Innes composts or soil mixtures. These are not a proprietary product, but were devised by scientists at the John Innes Research Institute. They are, in fact, merely a special soil prepared to a standard recipe and can generally be bought from all nurseries, garden centres and indeed from many chain stores. They have certain distinct advantages, which is why they are recommended. In the first place, there are several types, for sowing seeds, for potting plants, for taking cuttings. Secondly, if they are correctly made, they are standard and will not vary in strength. Thirdly, the soil content has been partially sterilised, which means that all weed seeds in them have been heat-killed. So if you sow some seed in John Innes (frequently shortened to JI) Seed Compost you will know that the tiny green leaves appearing are those of the germinated seed you have sown rather than some unknown weed. JI mixtures are available ready bagged in small or large quantities. It is possible to make your own from the standard recipes, but as this involves the purchase of a soil steriliser the expense is not generally justified.

In the past few years a number of other composts have appeared on the market, most of them doing without soil because of the problem of sterilisation and consequently known as 'no-soil' composts or

ground and rotted. We can make our own good soil on the same principle and this soil will be better in many ways than anything we can buy. For this reason the bonfire should be used only for tap-rooted weeds and for woody material which will take too long to decompose. Everything else from the garden should go on the compost heap. This will include waste vegetable matter from the kitchen, grass cuttings, hedge trimmings, fallen leaves and even the contents of the vacuum cleaner bag.

The compost heap is made in an open topped 'box' with sides sufficiently open to allow some air through. (You can buy ready made bins. You can also use metal netting.) If one side is removable it is so much more convenient, but this is not essential. Dimensions depend on the size of the garden and hence the quantity of the material at hand, but generally it should be at least 3 feet square. At the base, lay at least 6 inches of fairly heavy twiggy material so that some air is allowed to pass under the heap and so that moisture can get away easily. Then on this base the compost heap proper can be started. All green vegetable matter should be thrown into the bin or box and when there is a layer some 6 to 9 inches deep it should be covered with a couple mixtures. Based on peat, these are clean to handle, light in weight, sterile, capable of absorbing many times their own weight in water and generally bringing a new ease and certainty to seed sowing and taking cuttings.

But obviously the extent to which you use the latest scientific aids in your garden must necessarily depend on the amount you wish to spend and the size of your garden. It is perfectly possible to have a most beautiful garden without the use of any of them. Perhaps the best advice I can give to gardeners is that they should obtain a good and comprehensive catalogue of garden sundries. From this it can be seen at a glance what products exist and the price can then be balanced against the value of the produce in your own garden.

Vegetables

The kitchen plot has been banished from many gardens, mainly because it often appears so unattractive. Yet this need not be so. Why, for example, grow the long-suffering Brussels sprouts directly outside the kitchen window when you could, instead, look out on a fruit and herb border planted to screen the less prepossessing plants beyond?

Much depends on how many vegetables you wish to grow. If you need only a few, grow those which are expensive at certain times, or difficult to get from the nearest shop. Often they can be set among the flowers, used as edgings to paths or borders, as patterns in a patio. You would be surprised to see how prettily and inconspicuously they can be made to blend if you give your mind to it.

One friend of mine has no defined vegetable plot at all, yet she manages to grow a wavy line of spinach behind a row of pinks, alpine strawberries along another border among low-growing flowers, lettuce, mint and parsley elsewhere. A great root of rhubarb fits extraordinarily well near the water garden and has become part of the scene.

In the garden of another friend, a few neat rows of raspberries and lettuce are well hidden behind the steep rockery which slopes down to a pool. Few people who admire the splashing, romantic waterfall realise that behind it is a very matter-of-fact plot, imaginatively hidden.

In a reader's garden I visited in Northumberland, a lush plot of potatoes and cabbage near a summerhouse was screened by a hedge of pink roses. The blue-green of the brassicas looked most attractive, shining low down through the sugar-pink flowers.

One year, a chemical company asked my husband and me to design a 'His and Hers Garden' for their trade stand at Chelsea Flower Show. Mine was intended to show just how prettily yet thickly one could grow herbs, vegetables, and salads among flowering plants and make a small garden really productive as well as pretty. In it one could see the variegated kale, which could be eaten or used in flower arrangements, growing next to regal lilies and purple pansies in delightful colour harmony. A border of alpine strawberries, attractive for all summer and autumn with white flowers and red fruits, grew before a row of asparagus peas, which have bright crimson red blooms and, later, delicious pods. These followed the border of the stepping-stone path at the side of which grew little 'rotational' plots of salads and vegetables. Tomatoes grew near the wall of the 'house' although this, in fact, was covered with a flowering quince. At the back of the narrow food border, espalier fruit trees were planted to hide the fence.

We are all so accustomed to seeing the red-flowered scarlet runners in allotments and gardens all over the country that we seldom think of the bean as being anything other than utilitarian, but actually it can be used in many lovely ways. In the first place, other varieties are more handsome than the scarlet runner and, I can assure you, carry beans you will find a great deal more delicious. The handsome Blue Coco climbing French bean is one of them. Don't be put off by the violet coloured beans! These cook greener than any other you are likely to have seen. They are more tender and buttery and do not need slicing – merely breaking into pieces. If you cut them young, you can cook them whole.

This productive plant should be used in a decorative way. Try it as a screen at one side of your patio to give you a little privacy in summer. Try it growing up strings on a white-washed wall with vivid nasturtiums below. Try it up tripods at the back of a flower border. Try it for vivid colour effect alternated with scarlet runners and white runners.

If you grow sugar peas you will also be growing a pretty plant for these, too, have purple flowers. You can get other purple peas and fancy beans, all of which cook to a lovely green or a buttery yellow.

Maize or sweet corn grows best in blocks not rows, so that the plants protect each other from the wind. Here, then, is a good vegetable to grow in groups to the back of the border, staying there until late summer when you will have other tall subjects in bloom.

Gardeners wanting to grow gourds and all the marrow family usually go in search of a mound over which the plants can scramble. Here they are often very much in the way. But why not, if the plants naturally trail and climb, use this habit to advantage? Here again is a handsome and most effective patio plant. Courgettes make neat, attractive plants. Try three on your patio, each one in place of a paving stone. You will have special vegetables to cook, splendid foliage and exotic flowers.

So, if you have an ornamental garden but would like to grow a few vegetables go ahead, but bear one thing in mind, if you have to dig to get at your crop, then it is not likely to be a practical one to mix. On the other hand, any vegetable which can be cut like cabbage, gathered like spinach and the loose leaf lettuces such as the oak-leaved Salad Bowl, pulled like radishes or young carrots, and beets (all of which, when they are sown, need no more than a scratched soil surface), can do no harm at all.

The vegetable garden proper should always be well defined with clear boundaries. These boundaries, as I have already stated, can be useful and filled with more than one kind of plant. Espalier fruit trees, a row of soft fruit, alpine strawberries or a herb row, some low-growing flowers interlaced with them, anything like this will be preferable to a strictly utilitarian hedge such as box or greedy privet.

Order is essential in the vegetable garden, for it saves time and trouble. When planting or sowing always use a line so that you grow straight rows of vegetables. I have found that a plastic-covered clothes line is very useful for it is white, so easily seen and cleaned and tough. Your rows, where convenient, should run from north to south.

Ideally, divide the crops into three types: brassicas, roots (potatoes, parsnips, carrots, beets) and the remainder (onions, peas, lettuce, spinach) and make sure that each group is grown in a different area

Courgettes (baby marrows) make unusual and productive bedding plants when grown among paving stones on a patio

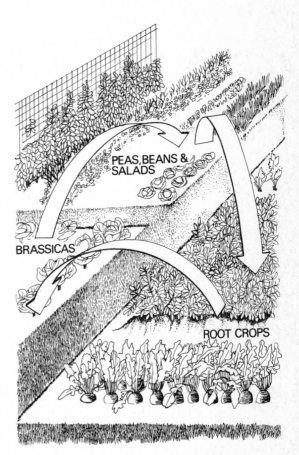

Correct three-year crop rotation can perhaps only be successfully operated in a large vegetable garden but this old-established and well-ordered system was designed to grow disease-free and succulent crops

65

each year. Those vegetables which should be most succulent and leafy – the peas, beans, lettuce and spinach – should go into the richest soil. Next year, the same soil will do for the roots and in the third year the plot, with possibly the addition of lime, should be used for the brassicas. This is the general rule for the effective rotation of crops.

But I feel that few of us have enough ground to be able to devote an entire patch to one type of vegetable and then to leave it empty when they have been cropped until the next year comes round. I don't follow strict, three-patch rotation but I do keep a clear plan so that I follow top-growth vegetables by tail-growth kinds.

If you have a tiny plot, you can divide it into four walking down to the middle from the centre of each side. Once you have these four squares with a path along all of them, you can also divide your crops, placing the neater-looking and quicker-maturing salad crops in the square most easily seen from house or ornamental garden. Place beans, Brussels and other long-standing crops further away. You can also arrange to empty one small plot and have it really well dug and manured and treat it in the way I described for rotational cropping. It would be a small plot but it need not remain empty for long.

Owners of freezers will find that they can clear a crop quicker than other gardeners, and the rotational type of cropping suits their purposes admirably.

As important as rotation and, I think, more practical in a small garden, is succession. One crop can follow another in many cases in the same year. To take only lettuce as an example, seed should be sown for succession as soon as the first sowing has germinated and is showing above the soil. This way, you are never without something for the summer salad bowl.

The catalogue from a good seedsman will help you greatly. Modern varieties of plants are such an improvement on the old ones. There are now small, compact types of cabbage, lettuce and other greens ideal for small gardens. Many newcomers are 'long-standing' which means that lettuce, for example, don't bolt to produce flower and seed quickly, and so a row will serve you over a much longer period than it used to. Cauliflowers can be timed to mature in a certain number of weeks. Cabbage keep a nice tight head and take little space.

Choose seed of varieties which suit your purpose. For example, you probably know early in the year the date of your holiday, so try not to select or sow seed which will mature at this time. Choose instead earlier or later varieties.

Order your seed in plenty of time, and prepare your soil as early as you can so that as soon as the season is right you can go into action. Choose a dry day for your seed sowing. Treat each seed as a potential plant. Where you can handle the seed, sow it singly. Thick-sown is wasted seed.

It really is worthwhile to invest in cloches even if you have no more than enough to make one row across your garden. By using mine I find that all through winter I have fresh salad of lamb's lettuce, sometimes called corn salad, winter radish, land cress which is very much like watercress, lettuce and endive. These, mingled with shredded savoy or Brussels sprouts, give one a great variety in raw vegetables at a time when they are very expensive in the shops. Money saved this way will soon help to pay for cloches.

After having protected plants in winter, the cloches can be moved along to warm and slightly dry the soil for early seed sowing and planting. They can be placed over early potatoes, peas, lettuce and carrots and, when they have served their turn here, they can be moved over the strawberries to protect them from the birds. Alternatively, you can use them to force the strawberries to fruit early by covering them with cloches in February. You can then use them to provide warmth for all kinds of gourds (marrow family) sown or planted outdoors. Stood on end securely, they will protect tomatoes on the cool or windy side of plants. One word of warning, do not place cloches near fruit trees where windfalls can damage the glass.

If you have no cloches or garden frames you can give half-hardy or tender seedlings, including small tomato plants, protection by using a two-pound jam-jar or a transparent plastic vessel of some kind. Merely place the jar over tiny individual plants. To sow all gourds outdoors, press the cover in the soil to indicate the area, remove a little of the soil in the centre and replace with some of better quality should this be necessary. Sow the seeds and cover tightly with the jam-jar. This is an excellent way of sowing courgettes set in rows across the garden. Do not remove the cover until all fear of frost is passed. Do not remove it to water the plants. They should be quite all right.

Some vegetables, like other annuals, are sown where they are to mature. These should be sown very thinly if they are small seeds. If they are large enough to handle, such as peas, it is possible roughly to space them, but I never go to the trouble of doing this precisely.

Generally speaking new gardeners grow vegetables too thickly and ardent and keen gardeners, usually the men gardeners (forgive me, gentlemen!) allow so much space between plants and rows that the vegetable garden is quite uneconomic in these days of high land prices. What is worse is that the resulting vegetables are usually big and coarse, hard to prepare and unsatisfactory to cook.

The most important factor in successful vegetable culture is quick growth, for this gives tenderness and flavour. This means that the soil must be good.

Although many plants do not need to be as widely spaced as is often recommended, it really is important to thin out all seedlings, even if you have sown thinly in the first place. You can cut out a certain amount of work in some cases by sowing at 'stations' certain distances apart, rather than in a long unbroken line. A pinch of parsnip or spinach seed, for example, is best sown at intervals 4 inches apart. If you want whopper parsnips, make it 8 inches. Some people fill in the spaces between with radish for pulling long before the others crowd them, or with lettuce to thin out later. Remember that crowded root vegetables become stringy and tough.

Thinnings of all leaf vegetables may be transplanted, but not many people bother to transplant spinach or spinach beet. Thinnings of these, after all, can be cooked even if they are very small. Lettuce transplanted after late May and early June tends to bolt. It is best to sow thinly and thin out.

One should always thin out when the soil is moist, after a shower is a good time. Press down the soil with the hand if it becomes disturbed. Look for the largest plants and thin out the puny ones among them. Do not thin out in one operation, because this disturbs the roots too much. Go back two or three times to thin, but do not leave too long an interval between this. Carrots, spinach and beet can be thinned first to 1 inch, then as the plants grow thicker and touch each other, alternate plants can be removed and so on.

Plants which need to be strong and sturdy, such as all the brassicas, usually should be moved two or three times, although it is possible to sow cabbage thinly, to thin out and to allow the plants to mature where they stand. This is a good way of ensuring succession, for the thinnings can be transplanted either from the row or first pricked out into nursery beds. When these have formed five or six leaves and a good fibrous root system, they can be planted in their permanent positions.

It is always difficult to know just how many seeds to buy. Some are sold by the ounce, half ounce or

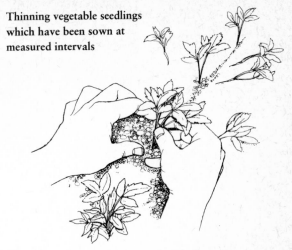

Thinning vegetable seedlings which have been sown at measured intervals

quarter ounce. After that they become packets of various sizes. Seed is cheaper by the ounce but usually far too much for a small garden. You could share packets with your neighbours, of course. You will probably be surprised to find just how many plants you have from a small packet. Here is a rough guide. Remember you need to save some seed of early crops for successive sowing. Do not try to save your own seed. It just is not worth it.

For a row roughly 50 feet long (I am allowing for the fact that many of you will sow far too thickly!) you need $\frac{1}{8}$ ounce lettuce, $\frac{1}{6}$ ounce onion, $\frac{1}{4}$ ounce parsley, $\frac{1}{2}$ pint broad or runner beans and $\frac{1}{4}$ pint French or haricot beans, $\frac{1}{4}$ pint peas, 7 pounds potatoes, $\frac{1}{2}$ ounce radish, $\frac{1}{4}$ pound shallots, $\frac{1}{4}$ ounce spinach and beet, $\frac{1}{4}$ ounce turnip and swede, 1 ounce of sweet corn, $\frac{1}{4}$ ounce carrots. Small packets of most other vegetables should do.

Increasing numbers of seeds are now available in pelleted form. The coating contains protective substances to aid germination and the larger size permits single sowing.

I fear that many of the rules for vegetable gardening were laid down in the past by people who worked under different conditions from today's. We are often shown pictures of a drill for peas being drawn out by pulling a hoe through the soil, apparently very easily. My soil is not light enough for me to do it this way and neither, I suspect, is the soil in many other gardens. Consequently drawing a deep drill can be a lengthy as well as hard job. I prefer to use my small border fork for this operation. I merely work along the line, removing the soil to the required depth and levelling the bottom of the drill with the fork as I go.

So long as the soil is prepared, you can by-pass many arduous and time-consuming jobs. Beans may be dibbled in; potatoes planted with the trowel.

Actually, if you are prepared to spend a little extra money, potatoes can be set on the top of the soil and merely covered along the rows with black polythene, which should be weighted down with soil along its margins. When you see that the potato shoots are pushing up the plastic, cut a slit to allow the foliage to grow through to the daylight. This way you will not even have to dig the potatoes, or the whole root either, because you merely help yourself to the tubers lying under their black cover. I have grown potatoes successfully this way but I dislike it for two reasons. One, the plastic has to be renewed annually and I try to cut expense to the minimum when producing vegetables, otherwise, one might as well buy them! And two, I prefer to dig up the tubers, because this is often all the digging that the soil in the row area gets before a top crop follows the roots.

Actually, potatoes are not a very economic crop for a small garden. I grow no maincrops at all, just a few of the early varieties, because no potatoes one buys have quite the same flavour as those grown in one's own garden and cooked with home-grown mint.

Although I always sow some onion seed, mainly to provide spring or salad onions, I also grow sets, small onion bulbs, for my main crop. These are far less work than seed and certainly more satisfactory for the amateur gardener. These sets and shallot bulbs (shallots, by the way, are vegetables you could hide among the flowers) give one a good opportunity of getting the garden going early in the year. The green spears begin to show in about three or four weeks. Usually, one is advised merely to press the bulbs in the soil but they become moved, not by birds, but by worms and even slugs. Mine, grown now in a bird-proof cage, become moved as much as any which grow outside.

Try this as a way to avoid the nuisance of having to go back and press the bulbs into their original stations. Draw out a very shallow drill. Press the bulbs in this and cover all but the very tip and firm them slightly. The bulbs tend to lift themselves a little as they grow and finally you will find them at soil level.

Herbs

The use of herbs seems to have become surrounded by an aura of mystery, or worse still, misplaced sophistication. Yet once every good garden, including little plots, had its herb patch – until recently almost a rarity, but now returning to favour.

These aromatic, attractive, useful and quite often health-giving plants deserve their rightful place in every garden. What herbs you grow will depend upon your tastes in food and cooking, even if you do not use all of them you will find many which are worth growing for their scent and character.

Well-planned, a herb plot can be as pretty as a picture, not so flamboyant as a herbaceous border, but with a charm of its own. Almost all herbs have flowers, and many are evergreen. You can either set aside a definite patch (perhaps where the evening light from the open kitchen door falls on them, so you will have them at hand when the unexpected guest stays to a meal), or use grouped herbs as a border along the vegetable garden path. In a small garden you can grow them in a mixed or shrub border with cushiony, bushy plants like thyme in the foreground. Some, like rosemary, fennel (that handsome feathery plant in green or bronze with green-yellow umbels that look so good with blue delphiniums or autumn flowers), borage (as blue and hazy as a summer day), sage, coriander, marjoram, may be planted in the mixed border to save room and provide interest, while the gardener with a collector's instinct can create a patch full of character, pungency and subtle colour. Most herb flowers are green, lavender or pink. Nearly all provide winter decoration in the garden.

If, on a country walk, you have found wild herbs, such as purple thyme growing, you will know that these plants like a hot sun-baked situation. This applies to most garden herbs too. They like light, well-drained soil that's not very rich. Heavy soil affects their pungency! Exceptions are the mints or mentha, including peppermint and pennyroyal, which seem to do almost anywhere, and angelica, which likes moist shade. Parsley and chervil like moist, fertile soil.

Like other garden plants, herbs are annual, biennial or perennial. Some are best grown from seed, and although most of the others may be grown this way also it is often more practical and economical in the long run to buy one mature plant rather than to spend roughly the same money on one packet of seed which will give so many plants to care for that they prove an embarrassment.

Best grown as annuals are anise, basil, borage, caraway, chervil, coriander, cumin, dill, parsley, sweet marjoram, sorrel and summer savory. Most of the shrubs, including those like sage, rosemary and hyssop, can be grown from heeled cuttings. Many others, like lavender, are grown for scent, not eating.

Herbs which are used in quantity are best grown in rows, either along a path or across the vegetable patch or in good-sized groups (sow the seed inside a circle in the border). Such herbs include parsley, chervil, chives, Florence fennel and sorrel. Allow plenty of space between the plants, so that you can gather them easily or group very dwarf-growing kinds among the taller ones.

Some, especially mint, are inclined to wander by means of string-like over-exploring roots. To confine these, plant them in a bottomless bucket or a box sunk in the soil, its rim on a level with the surface.

Mints, or mentha, are more varied than many people realise. *M. spicata* is the one most widely grown and offered for sale yet it is nothing like so good in flavour as the woolly leaves of *M. rotundifolia*. Beg a root of this if you see it growing anywhere. It is quite unmistakable.

For drying, herbs should be gathered when the flowers have just opened fully and are at their best. Annual green and evergreen herbs may also be dried, but are best used fresh. By protecting them with cloches, by sowing seed in succession, or by lifting one or more of a certain kind and growing them in a frame, or in pots or boxes in a greenhouse, or even on a sunny window-sill you can have fresh herbs in the winter.

You can force mint for winter sauce. Fill a box or some large pots with roots which look like (and are) underground stems. Cut them in pieces and just cover with soil and bring into a warm greenhouse or a warm window-sill in relays. Keep the soil moist, and if warm enough, sprigs can be cut after three weeks.

Parsley seed needs to be sown every other year for a continuous supply, although you can, of course, make a fresh sowing each year.

There are three recommended seasons for sowing, February, May and July, but you should use your discretion and sow according to seasonal conditions. I find that August is often a good time, July sometimes being cold and wet.

The seeds take a long time to germinate so do not worry if they do not appear for five or six weeks. Sow a few radish seed in the shallow drills along with the parsley seed. These will come up quickly and so keep you reminded that there is a crop to come.

Sow the seed thinly. You may need only a small packet; a quarter ounce, for example, is sufficient for a 50-foot row. Thin out to 2 or 3 inches apart when the parsley plants show their first curly leaf. Later on thin plants to 6 to 8 inches apart. You can transplant the thinnings. Keep the leaves continually cut to induce the plants to keep growing.

We expect parsley to be green and curly; Fine Moss Curled, in fact, is a seed catalogue term. The French parsley is nothing like so attractive in appearance yet its flavour is far superior; it is good for drying and keeps greener. Hamburg parsley has similar foliage to French which can be used in the same way but its succulent roots may be cooked like parsnips. They are smaller but finer in flavour and make a good crop for the small kitchen garden.

Chervil is similar to parsley in appearance. It goes to flower much more rapidly, being an annual and for this reason should be sown in succession. I sow it at fortnightly intervals through summer, demolishing one crop when the next is ready. A pinch of seed gives many plants. They can be transplanted, but this checks growth.

Chives, like many other bulbous plants, are best lifted and divided frequently. Given a good soil and plenty of sun, they will grow surprisingly well and provide leaves until late autumn, so long as these are cut frequently. Flowers can be eaten. Lift and divide plants in spring, pulling them apart and replanting smaller portions. You can grow chives in a pot outside on the window-sill but remember to water it often.

Thyme will grow anywhere, except in heavy clay. The plant loves sunshine and looks delightful scrambling over the edge of a sun-baked stone, or even cement, path. Plant in spring and replant every three or four years.

Sage, too, will grow in ordinary soil, but given a sunny, dryish spot, it will grow into a fine bush. It should be planted in late spring. I have one three years old and three feet through.

It pays to fuss over a sage plant in its first year, watering well in hot dry weather and nipping out the young tips to encourage bushiness. Old plants sometimes become very leggy. When this happens, the plant should be renewed by seed sown in heat in March or by cuttings taken in a frame in April. Or, if like me you have 'green toes', try pulling off a shoot from the plant and firmly heeling it into the soil.

Originally from the tropics, sweet basil is a half-hardy annual. Seeds should be sown in a greenhouse, pricked out and hardened off before planting outdoors as with any other half-hardy annual. When they are first put into the soil, see that the young plants are shaded from the sun or they may quickly dry up. Keep them well watered. Gather the tips and leaves when coming into flower, dry and powder.

Pot marjoram, will grow anywhere, but really needs sun to do its best. Plants need not be divided each year, but they do benefit from an annual dressing of manure.

Rosemary is a delightful shrub which, in a sheltered garden, will grow high, wide and handsome, as visitors to the Channel Islands and all points south will know. In winter and early spring, the stems are studded with blue flowers. It will grow in ordinary soil and, so I have found, in a windy spot, but in hot weather it should never be allowed to become dry. Plant in April.

Summer savory is a hardy annual. Seed may be sown in a sunny spot directly into the soil. Thin the seedlings to 6 inches apart. Give plenty of water in dry weather. Pull the plants when they are in flower and hang for winter use.

Tarragon is related to lad's love, wormwood and other pungent artemisias. Ordinary soil will do so long as it is dry and in a sunny spot. Plant in spring and divide each year. Cuttings may be taken and struck in a temperature of 13°C. (55°F.). The leaves should be cut at the end of summer and dried. From an infusion of these, we can make tarragon vinegar. Like the mint, a few roots may be boxed or potted and brought into a warm greenhouse in October to produce succulent shoots during winter.

All these plants should be gathered for drying when the plants are in flower, for then the leaves will be quite mature. Young shoots are too succulent for drying. Choose a fine day to gather them. I like to feel them sun-warm. Divide them into small bunches, cut off dead and dying leaves and any pieces of root. Wash thoroughly, later drying off

with a cloth. String the bunches on sticks for easy handling. Hang them in a hot greenhouse, in a still-warm oven, before a fire or in an airing cupboard.

When the leaves are dry enough to be no longer soft to the touch, tie each bunch in a paper or polythene bag to protect it from dust with the stems at the open end, and hang in a dry place.

Borage is mainly used in its fresh state. The sprigs are used to flavour fruit cup or individual leaves can be dipped in batter and fried. Once sown in March in a sunny spot, it will reseed itself every year. You will need to thin out the young plants rigorously. The plant is a pretty one with really blue flowers.

Some herbs grow very large and some can become a nuisance. You can take advantage of the size of some of them. Angelica, for example, is such a handsome plant architecturally that it really deserves to be grown where it can be admired towering against the skyline. If you have a water garden, it will look well in this vicinity. It will also look well in a courtyard; and you can be happy that if the children want to use its hollow stems as pea shooters, they will be quite safe. Unlike many wild plants of this family this is not poisonous. The *Umbelliferae* provides us with many vegetables and herbs, but do not assume that because one part of the plant is wholesome all parts are. This is not the case. Parsnip roots are good but their leaves and seeds should not be eaten. Coriander, caraway, dill and parsley seeds can be used as flavouring but one should not try the others; they may not be poisonous but it is best to be sure.

Horseradish is much esteemed but do hesitate before you plant it in the garden because it can become a troublesome weed, and don't allow perennial fennel to drop its seed or plants will pop up unexpectedly in the wrong places.

Bunches of herbs hanging up to dry in a warm greenhouse.

Fruit

No matter how small your garden, you can grow some fruit. Fruit trees can be decorative as well as utilitarian so that they may be incorporated into the flower garden if you have no kitchen garden. This way, you get double value. No matter what type of tree you choose, you will have blossom in the spring as well as handsome fruit later and perhaps a little lovely leaf colour in the autumn.

If you have no spare space in your borders, you can use the walls of your house, or dividing fences, or dividing wires, even the area overhead over garden paths and patios. On a warm west, southwest or south wall you can train pear, peach, nectarine, apricot or grape, figs, choice plums and apples. On the north and east, you can grow Morello cherries, cordon and trained gooseberries and currants and hardy plums. Blackcurrants and the piquant-flavoured quince will grow in damp areas.

By planting more than one kind of tree, you can have a succession of blossom to make your garden look really lovely in spring. By careful selection of varieties, you can get blossom you most like and fruit most suited to your purpose. Plum blossom is snowy white and comes very early, often long before any of the blossoming shrubs which you have planted especially for the effect of their flowers. Peach blossom is also very early, rosy, prolific and beautiful and it often blooms with the yellow forsythia. Pear follows and, much later, comes the apple with pink-backed blooms. Some are much rosier than others; James Grieve, which has sharp, juicy fruits in the autumn, has richly coloured flowers like single pink roses. Bramleys probably produce the prettiest picture when in full blossom, and trees grow large enough to give romantic shade on a lawn or patio. Its fruit will also keep until Easter.

On the other hand, if you are looking for something to give you a light and attractive screen, perhaps at the end of the garden to shut out or mask an unsightly view, a closely-planted row of pyramid-trained apples or pears, or perhaps half and half, only 6 feet apart, will be ideal for this purpose. I once saw a courtyard entirely roofed with grape vines trained to a system of metal arches.

If you have a large garden, Conference pear is good for shade. An avenue of cherries along the drive makes a pretty sight and gives fruit into the bargain. Plums and damsons make a good windbreak. Blackberries, wineberries and loganberries can be used to cover a shed or to disguise an old tree.

Raspberries can be grown along the side of a path where the paving will keep them from trespassing as they are inclined to do. Currants take little room because they have to be well pruned every year. Alpine strawberries can be grown as a ground cover or as an edging. New varieties give you large, delicious fruits which go on and on. In my family, we are often eating bowls of strawberries and cream in late November. The other types of strawberries can now be chosen to give you a selection that will take you on into November. If you grow strawberries in strict rows and not in an impractical bed, you will have little work. Three rows are needed, the oldest which has been allowed to fruit for three years only, being discarded annually and replaced by a row of young plants raised from runners taken from the youngest and most vigorous row.

I never put straw down around my plants. I did at one time, but now I have another method of keeping them clean and helping them to ripen. As soon as the fruits begin to swell, I place slug pellets along the row (one finds too many slug-hollowed fruits if this precaution is not taken) and I also dust the soil with ant powder at intervals. The row of plants is then covered with a strip of clear polythene, which is weighed down at the edges. This actually rests on and touches the plants, but because it is at ground level no burning of the foliage results. The first time I did this, it was so successful that I tried it on the raspberry rows (at that time we had no fruit cage, and birds were taking too many of the berries) but all the young autumn-fruiting canes became scorched, no doubt because, being so far from the soil, they were not, like the strawberries, kept cool. Alpine strawberries are treated in the same way. When you come to pick the fruits, it is a simple matter to turn the plastic back, and then to replace it when picking is finished.

But to return to the ordinary type of strawberry. I know that correct horticultural practice recommends that one should remove all the flowers from the plants during the first year so that the second year's crop will be heavier than the first and second together. Quite frankly I doubt whether the probable quantity of fruit in the following year is sufficient compensation for missing the first year's crop. All I can tell you is that, rightly or wrongly, I have never removed the bloom from my strawberry plants but have always let them fruit. However, and I cannot stress this too much, I do believe it is essential to feed the plants well. While many soils suit strawberries, very dry soils and very limy ones do not.

Strawberries suffer from a certain virus, and so it is essential to buy from a reputable source where plants will be given a Special Stock Certificate. Although planting can be carried out in spring, autumn is the better time. If you can be sure that the plants will be watered and cared for, it is also quite all right to plant in July and August.

Once you have your own plants, they may be increased by the runners produced by the parent plants. More runners than are needed will be produced, so the surplus should be cut off as soon as they are seen and not allowed to grow and root. As I grow mine on the three row system already explained, I increase the stock as simply as possible. A line across the plot is placed $2\frac{1}{2}$ feet from the youngest row. Runners are directed from the plants to reach the line and spaced out between a foot and 15 inches apart along it. Usually, I anchor them down with a lump of soil placed on the stolon. I also scatter a little peat along the line to stimulate rooting and to give the young plants a little acid soil to begin with. Once the row is filled, all the other runners made by the plants in the three rows are cut off so that the one row alone grows. Runners go on being produced until the early autumn so you need to keep watch on the plants all the time.

There is now a fine choice of varieties for the early crop including some varieties which do best under cloches and are good for freezing. The strawberry season can be extended by growing some of the Remontants which come into production from August onwards. There are several varieties and the flavour is a little different from the early type.

I used to grow alpine strawberry Baron Solemacher which is delicious, but I have transferred my affections to Alexandria which retains the delicate, almost banana-like flavour and texture but which has much larger fruits. Both of these varieties can be raised from seed. Germination is erratic, so after pricking out seedlings, retain and care for the box or pot for some weeks and more seedlings are almost certain to appear. Fruit may be picked the first year from seed if you sow early in the season. Later on as they grow big, plants can be divided.

The so-called climbing strawberry is attractive grown in hanging baskets or a strawberry barrel, but it makes a better ground cover plant and can be grown in a separate bed or among shrubs.

Raspberries are good fruit for most soils but, like strawberries, these do not like light, dry soils. In dry seasons on dryish soils, you will find that it considerably improves the crop if, as soon as the fruit is set, you water the ground very well. I keep my own raspberries, Lloyd George a 'perpetual' fruiting variety, heavily mulched with grass mowings in summer and manure in autumn and winter and I gather fine fruits up until November. Peak crop is in June-July. There are many good varieties.

Plant any time from mid-October until March. However, if the season is moist and the need urgent, I have found that planting can be done at almost any time. So if you are moving house, don't hesitate to take canes with you, but make sure that you lift plenty of soil and keep the roots from becoming dry.

Raspberries, planted 2 feet apart grow into clumps and subsequently join up in rows. New canes push up from the ground and are inclined to wander and cause the row to widen and spread. I keep mine under control by mulching the area lavishly beyond the row's limits with fresh lawn mowings. This keeps down weeds, enriches the soil and prevents the young canes pushing up in this area. One can hoe them off, pull or dig them up when this is necessary. Raspberries root very near the surface so this should be disturbed as little as possible.

To keep the fruit on the heavily cropped canes off the ground each should be tied to wires stretched parallel along the rows from strong posts. The top wire should be 5 to 6 feet above ground level. Allow each plant to form five or six canes, and spread these apart, tying them to the wires.

Prune summer-fruiting varieties as soon as the canes have finished fruiting. Cut them to 6 inches above ground level. Young canes soon take their place. Keep long canes tipped, so that they do not tower too far above the top wire. Canes which have fruited in autumn should be cut back in February.

Blackberries, loganberries, wineberries and other hybrid berries all do well in ordinary garden soil but they dislike dry poor soils. They enjoy summer mulches – just think of the lush places where you find the best blackberries growing wild! Plant 8 feet apart; growth can be very vigorous. After fruiting, all spent canes should be cut to ground level and the young softer canes tied into their place. You will find it easiest to have double training wires, just a little apart from each other. Tie this year's canes to one layer of wires, and as the new canes form, tie these to the other. You will then find work less irritating when you come to prune. I find it best to snip the cane away in one- or two-foot portions, starting from the tip rather than to try to pull out the entire cane.

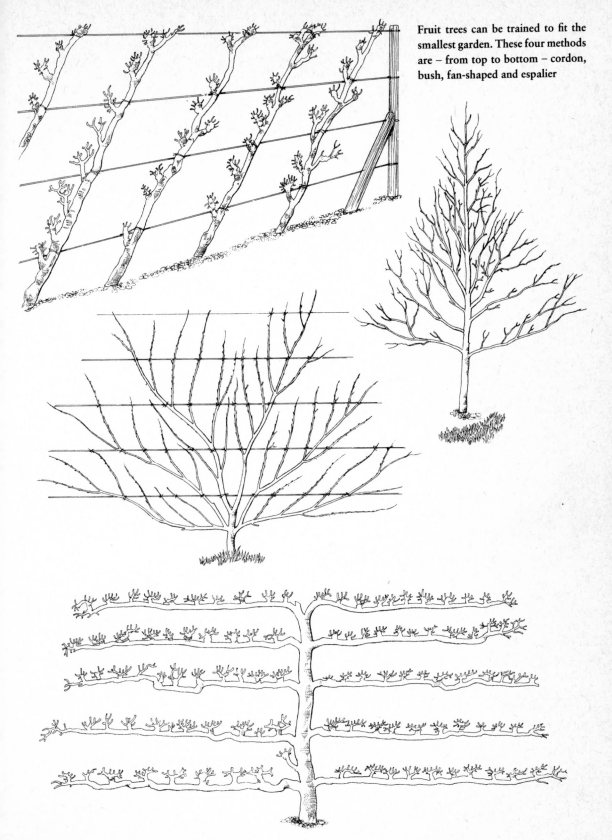

Fruit trees can be trained to fit the smallest garden. These four methods are – from top to bottom – cordon, bush, fan-shaped and espalier

73

Before ordering fruit, make sure you know what shape of tree or bush you wish to grow. Red, black and white currants and gooseberries are grown as bushes and should be planted about 4 feet apart. Gooseberries can also be successfully grown as cordons and planted closer. I have two blackcurrant bushes growing in a mixed border, simply because they happened to be there when we made the border, and we have never got round to moving them. They do very well, but they have to be netted against birds when the fruit is ripe unless I get there when the fruit is just colouring. Then I cut the branches and take them indoors and stand them in buckets of water until I am ready for them. In this way pruning is done at harvesting, a most convenient arrangement. All branches bearing fruit are cut and the berries can then be removed in comparative comfort. This is not the case with red and white currants, which are produced on the old wood and so cannot be harvested this way.

Blackberries, wineberries (greatly to be recommended if you don't know them – not only is the fruit good but the canes are handsome enough to be grown against a wall), and loganberries need 10 feet between the plants. After the first growth these will produce strong-growing canes which should be tied on to wires or a framework. These canes can be trained to run horizontally. I grow mine inside the kitchen garden cage, tied to the wires which support the wire-netting walls.

If you hope to grow a good crop of various fruits, you need to choose the varieties carefully. Some trees, which we call self-fertile, bear blossom which fertilises its own flowers. But there are others that will not set fruit unless pollen from another tree of the same kind is available. If no tree is close you can gather a flowering branch from one a distance away and set it in a jar of water pushed into the ground near your own tree.

In fact, it is not wise to plant an apple by itself, for even the self-fertile varieties are improved by cross pollination. Apple blossom opens at different times, so one needs to choose varieties that will be in blossom simultaneously. When you go to a nurseryman to choose your fruit, he will advise you which are good cross pollinators to plant with the varieties you particularly want. In good catalogues this is also pointed out.

If you have an old-established pear tree that is shy to fruit, it is wise to call in an expert who will graft on a new branch of a different variety to pollinate it.

If you are planning the garden, it is much better to plant fruit of the same kind near each other. But this does not necessarily mean that you must plant the same variety, for it makes no difference to the pollination if one is a cooking variety and one is a dessert.

If you intend growing a lot of fruit, bear in mind that you will need to plant a succession, otherwise everything will come at once. With a little planning you can extend the season. Apples will ripen from August onwards according to their varieties. There are some that can be kept as late as April. Pears mature from July to the New Year. Plums do not keep, but they will fruit in August, September or October.

You can buy different types of fruit trees. One-year-old trees are known as maidens, and you can train these into any form you wish. It is advisable, when ordering them, to tell the nurseryman how you intend to train them. Bush trees are useful for small gardens because you can pick fruit from them easily. But on the other hand a standard tree, that is one on a long trunk, will rise well above your flower borders and looks lovely as a special tree for a lawn. Standard trees are usually on 6-foot stems. Half standards are much shorter, usually about $4\frac{1}{2}$ feet. Espalier trees are like a ladder with a centre stem. Bush trees need to be about 12 feet apart for apples and pears but further apart for plums and other stone fruits. Pyramid trees, that is trees trained in a pyramid shape, can be grown as close as 6 feet.

The best space savers are cordon trees. These are grown on one stem only (this is the sort of thing you buy a maiden tree for) and you can plant cordons as close as $3\frac{1}{2}$ feet. Don't attempt to grow cordon trees unless you are a keen gardener, for you must keep them well pruned in winter and in summer.

Best for walls are fan-trained trees, and fan training particularly suits the stone fruits, including peaches, nectarines and apricots.

A few pence more in the price you pay will enable you to get plants from the best growers in the country. And going to the best nurserymen will give you further practical advantages such as expert advice. Send a sample of your soil when ordering so that the best plants on the most suitable rootstock can be chosen for you.

Do accept this expert advice. England's gardens are crammed (to take only one example) with Cox's Orange Pippin trees that will never do well because they are in a cold wet soil or a hot dry one.

Any soil that will grow weeds will grow fruit, with the possible exception of pure chalk. But this doesn't mean that soils need not be improved.

The greatest danger with fruit is waterlogging, so if your soil is heavy, with a clay subsoil, dig deep to loosen the lower layers before planting. If your soil is very badly drained, dig deeply (at least 2 to 3 feet), bury some large stones, half bricks or large clinkers in the base, cover with at least 6 inches of soil and then work on this base.

A very light sandy soil again presents difficulties. In this case, incorporate good leafmould, rich compost or well-rotted manure in the planting holes. In other words, enrich the humus-making content of the soil.

Some fruit will grow almost anywhere in this country, but some varieties are susceptible to frost damage. Do not plant fruit (unless you have reason to know local conditions) until you have experienced one spring and winter or have taken local advice.

Stone fruits generally are grown as standards, half-standards or bushes, for they fruit on young wood and intensive pruning for shape is death to the crop! In fact, one sees so much bad pruning that I am tempted to say to the novice, 'don't bother if you don't know'. Stone fruits though may be fan trained (usually they are bought ready trained) and this makes them convenient plants to grow flat against a wall or fence. Pruning here consists in retaining the fan outline but filling it with young fruiting shoots. Those that are growing naturally to one side or another are tied, as soon as they are large enough, to guide wires stretched across the wall, about a foot apart, one above the other. Obviously, shoots which tend to grow outwards are an embarrassment. These are 'rubbed out' when they are quite young to prevent them developing.

Fruit trees are not grown commercially from seeds or cuttings but good varieties are grafted on to several types of rootstock. Some stocks are dwarfing, some vigorous. It is not necessary here to go deeper into this somewhat complex matter except to urge that when buying fruit trees all relevant information should be given to the supplier so that he can choose the right rootstock for your own particular soil, situation and requirement. Obviously, in a small garden dwarfing stocks are best.

Fruit can be planted at any time between November and the end of March. Principles are exactly the same as for all tree and shrub planting except that on heavy soils rather more attention should be given to obtaining good drainage.

If there is room in the garden, it is best to grow apples in grass. This way they get a better colour, because potash is more accessible. Dress the grass in February with sulphate of ammonia and potash, roughly one ounce of each to the square yard. Initial planting should be in a small bed or circle of cleared land about 4 feet in diameter, which should be kept clear for the first two years. After this time, the trees should be well established and grass may be allowed to grow up to the stem. If fruit is grown on cleared land it should receive annual mulches of grass cuttings, decayed manure, good compost or leafmould. These mulches may be quite thick, I have seen them a foot deep, but should not be allowed actually to touch the tree or bark or they are likely to start a form of stem rot.

MORE ON PRUNING

Summer pruning – Apples The summer pruning of fruit trees and bushes is very important. Its purpose is to inhibit the production of more shoots and to channel the plant's energies into the production of fruit buds. The leaders are ignored and should never be shortened in summer. But we do shorten the long leafy laterals which then produce short clusters of fruit buds, known as spurs. Sometimes these spurs are formed by the end of the summer. If the pruning is done at the correct stage in the lateral's growth, you should be able to see the fruit buds formed immediately below the cut made when pruning. Sometimes, the buds do not form until the next year.

It is difficult to give exact dates for summer pruning, because so much depends upon locality as well as on the variety to be pruned. But generally, this is decided by the condition of the laterals. These should already be woody at the base and the leaves should be well developed. Laterals whose leaves are soft and sappy are not mature enough. If immature laterals are cut, the bushes will be induced to shoot again and so the purpose of pruning will be defeated. It is best not to attempt to prune the whole of a plant in one go but to return to it time and time again, pruning only those laterals which are ready.

Apples, cordon trained These should have all mature laterals growing directly from the main stem cut back to about three leaves. Mature shoots are usually 9 inches or more in length with a woody base and dark green leaves. Sometimes these laterals produce sub-lateral shoots which have grown from points below the cut made at a previous summer pruning (often because conditions were not quite right when this was done). Look for the basal cluster of leaves, and cut back to one leaf beyond it. Espalier trees should be pruned as for cordons.

Summer pruning – Pears Generally treated as for

75

apples, except that they are usually ready for pruning about mid-July. Apples are ready about two weeks later.

Winter pruning of Apples and Pears – Bushes, standards and half standards should be pruned so as to keep the centre of the tree open and enable light and air to get to it. Bushes can be gradually trained into a goblet shape with an open centre. Follow always the golden rule of winter pruning: prune hard to get strong growth, prune lightly to discourage growth. Always make a horizontal cut about one eighth of an inch above a bud which, for main branches, should always point away from the tree. Remove all strong growths going into the centre. Professional growers train youngsters to prune 'so you can throw your hat through the tree.'

Dwarf pyramids should have a central stem with branches radiating in a natural spiral – like a pyramid or triangle. Aim always to maintain this shape.

Cordons are planted and tied to canes or supporting wires at an angle of 45 degrees. Plant rows running north and south. When leaders reach the top wire, the entire cordon can be loosened from the training wires and lowered slightly, still keeping the plants parallel. Tip prune leaders by about one third each winter and thin spurs. For cordons, summer pruning is more important.

Gooseberries and Red and White Currants – Summer pruning Whether these are grown as bushes or cordons the method of pruning is virtually the same. Treat each branch as though it were a separate plant, a single-stemmed cordon. Every sideshoot growing from each branch must be cut back to allow about five leaves to remain.

So far as gooseberries are concerned, these can be most difficult to pick – one reason why a three part cordon is a good shape. But if you try to keep the branches off the ground so that you can get your hands below and thin the branches out so that you can get your hands between, you will find gathering the fruit easier.

Red and White Currants – Winter pruning This should be carried out between October and early February. This time laterals and leaders are pruned. Laterals are cut back so that only two or three buds remain on each. Cut leaders so that they are only one third as long.

Gooseberries – Winter pruning You have a chance now to trim the bush. Arching stems should be cut

back to an upright growing stem. Where leaders grow straight and very erect shorten them each time to a bud which points away from the centre of the bush. Remove any suckers.

SPRAYING

With all diseases, human and horticultural, it is helpful to attack them in the early stages. For this reason, winter fruit washes of tar oil or some proprietary substance are the most important. These washes should be thorough, drenching the trees, and should be carried out while the trees are dormant, between the beginning of December and the end of January. Tar oil will kill most aphid eggs, will clear bark of moss and lichen and remove many loose pieces of bark which harbour the pests. (It is also well worth spraying ornamental fruits such as prunus, amelanchier and pyrus.)

Good commercial growers spray more or less fortnightly from about March to July. We haven't time for this, but we should watch development and certainly spray with a fungicide such as lime sulphur or captan before bud burst (when the buds are green and tight clustered) and again with a fungicide and insecticide such as derris, lindane or malathion when the buds are just beginning to show colour. When the blossoms are actually open, the trees should be left severely alone both to save the lives of bees and other helpful pollinating insects and to avoid making the flowers distasteful to the bees. A further spray of fungicide and insecticide should be applied after petal fall.

There are many individual pests and diseases which can cause trouble in fruit. The main preventions and the main cures are contained in the winter tar oil washes and in spraying with insecticides and fungicides later in the year.

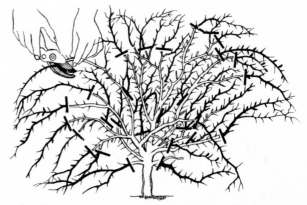

The winter pruning of a gooseberry bush

Restoring the neglected garden

Not everyone can begin from the beginning. You may be replanning an already established garden, trying to restore order to one which has been very neglected, or, like my husband and myself, be trying to make a garden from what was once a little paddock orchard and neglected hen-run.

From experience, I can tell you that one's aim here should be to create space first so that you have room to work. But do not rush this, for you may be sorry later. Remember that in saving an established tree you span the years it would take to plant your own and see it come to maturity.

In our own case, we had a great area of grass, not good lawn but a potential lawn, and by cutting it we were presented with a more than normal quantity of grass mowings. By this time we had planned what areas were eventually to be planted, and we decided to let the grass help us in our work. For instance, we needed a kitchen garden, and once the area was chosen the sparse grass and weeds that grew there were never collected but allowed to lie and rot where they fell. Here they stayed until the day came when we cultivated the plot. The deposits of vegetation on top of the 'turf' meant that successive mowings had given the patch of soil a deep humus content. Now vegetables and fruit grow rich and lush.

By letting the grass lie in certain other places – among newly planted trees, for example – we also relieved ourselves of the necessity of raking or collecting the mowings. Spare-minute gardeners need to be appreciative of what tasks can be left undone. We told ourselves that it would take 10 years of weekends (the only time we then had to spare) to achieve the effect we wanted and this has proved to be the case.

Although we had drawn up a plan for a rose garden and a grey border, the actual beds were not cut until we felt sure we could fit their cultivation into our routine. We just continued to pass the lawn mower over the area where these features would eventually be. The contents of the grass box were merely emptied on top of the growing grass, the low mound following the shape of the border we planned to make. The edges of the mound were kept compact and neat. When the grass was cut again, by which time the height of the mound had sunk considerably, more mowings were added. Soon, of course, the growing grass below was killed. Because the grass beyond the borders had been continually mowed, we were able to cut through it easily with a spade. This we did, following the outline of the border and throwing the turves on top of the mound. Later, these were covered with more mowings to suppress the grass and to reduce all to humusy soil. Meanwhile, we fell into the routine of using edging shears on the grass near the border to ensure that the lawn grass was kept from creeping into the part we were going to plant.

The important point was that at the beginning every one of our borders was very narrow. Having defined the area, we had to fill it with plants. Because time was so limited, it was more practical to plant a narrow space than a wide one. As both time and plants became available, the borders were easily widened.

From the psychological as well as the practical viewpoint, it is best to clear the ground gradually from the house to the boundaries rather than the other way round.

Not everyone is confronted with neglect or with creating order from a wilderness. Often a newcomer has no greater task than to reshape the garden according to personal preference. If possible keep trees and shrubs, for to replace mature growth here is expensive of time and you may have something better than you realise. Wait a season. Better, if possible, to plan your garden around any existing large tree. Many plants will grow quite happily in the shade of most trees.

If you must cut the tree down, you can either leave a stump for use as a table top or remove it entirely. To dig out a large stump is very hard work indeed. Better cut it down as near soil level as possible and then bore a series of holes in it. These should be at least an inch in diameter and 2 inches or so deep. Fill these with a solution of brushwood killer or sodium chlorate crystals. These will kill the roots and the stump will rot away.

Taking down and removing an established tree can be an arduous task and it can also be a dangerous one if the tree concerned is large. With a light saw, take off the top and the major branches, climbing up with the assistance of a ladder. Remove these from the base of the tree so you have space to move and work. If you are left with a tall naked stem, remove the main trunk in portions, about 2 or 3 feet long, for convenience.

When you are finally left with a trunk not more than 6 feet tall, you can begin excavating at the roots. Dig around the base of the tree, beginning not less

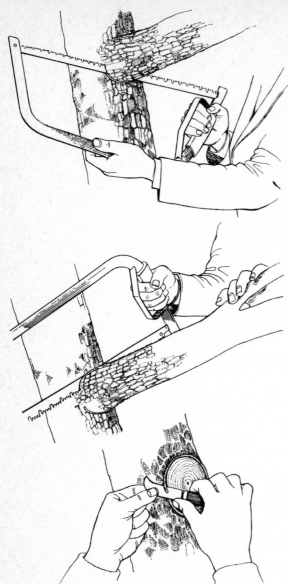

When removing a large branch make the first cut on the underside as close to the main branch as possible. Then sever the branch by sawing down from the top. Trim the wound before painting it with a sealing compound

than 2 or more than 6 feet from the trunk, depending on the size of the tree. Dig away the soil between the roots, placing it carefully aside in some place where it can eventually be used to refill the hole which will be left.

As you work, the major roots will be exposed. Chop these through in two places, next to the trunk and next to the perimeter, so you will have space to continue your digging. As these roots are removed, you will find that the trunk begins to move and can be rocked. The tall trunk now fulfils its purpose – to act as a lever. If this is tall, you will find that you can

rock it on the remaining roots and after several attempts you will find that the final roots will either be exposed or will be broken through by this rocking and eventually the trunk will fall. Saw this up and cart it away. Fill up the excavated hole left with the soil that was originally removed. This may settle after a few weeks and require levelling again with extra soil.

If you have trees which are not particularly decorative in themselves, but which you don't want to dig out, use them to support climbers grown naturally on them. For example, all kinds of clematis will grow up an apple tree. Honeysuckles, roses and flame flowers are just a few more. I have a red honeysuckle growing up and over a snowball tree, *Viburnum sterile*. When the white blossom has finished, the red honeysuckle takes over. Honeysuckles are very useful, but they like to be given a yearly mulch with leafmould, just as they would have if they were growing naturally in a wood. The Russian vine, with foamy white flowers, contrasts wonderfully with the colouring Virginia creeper in autumn. Try these two together over an old apple tree.

Few things sadden me more or make me more angry than the wanton mutilation of trees. Of course, trees that are far too large must be thinned; overhanging, barren and dead branches need removing but there is a right and wrong way. Simply, forgetting all about horticulture, you really cannot go far wrong if your ultimate aim is to leave the tree still a thing of beauty after treatment. Branches that need removing need taking right back close to the main trunk or limb. There should be no stump. If you can afford it, I recommend that you engage the services of a tree surgeon; estimates are given before work is undertaken. If you balance money you would have spent on trees with money spent on saving mature specimens, you will find that there is not much disparity.

Branches sawn right through from top to bottom will, as the saw reaches the end, fall off leaving a nasty snag. Often the fall pulls away bark from the main branch or trunk. Damaged bark leaves a tree susceptible to fungus attack and so must be avoided at all costs. Before beginning from the top of the branch, saw underneath making the cut upwards. Do this as close as possible to the main stem. Sawing is hard work. If you have no power tool it is worth trying to borrow or hire equipment.

Some conifers, but not all, which have grown too large can be cut back and retrained to take their characteristic shape. This applies to those whose branches grow upwards. The centre of the tree can be taken out to below the required height and the top branches tied to follow the natural shape.

Cypress-like conifers often become damaged by snow settling in their centres, and this pulls them out of shape but you can restore the shape by tying them like bundles, making several ties from tip to base. The trees look a little odd at first but they do improve. If they are trees which have to be clipped, wire ties may be used and left.

Shrubs which have got out of hand should be treated a little at a time if you need to reduce their area, as you would with an old hedge. It's worth going over the whole plant, removing crooked and spindly growths. Allow the strong vigorous parts to remain, but reduce their size. It is best to take away one portion right to ground level and then, should it still be necessary, to remove another part the following year.

Lilacs which have become a thicket of suckers often present a headache. There is nothing one can do about this if the growth is too rampant except dig up the lilac and the suckers with it. But if only a few suckers are seen, they should be traced back under the soil to the roots and cut off cleanly there with a sharp knife. It may be necessary to do this every few years. Heavy mulching around the base of a tree will help dissuade suckers, and careful spraying with a paraquat weedkiller can discourage their growth.

If you decide to keep and to try to renew apples and pears, be prepared to prune over several years and do not attempt it in one go. Almost certainly there will be dead wood. As pruning is best done in winter when there are no leaves on the tree, it will be wise to mark the dead wood with paint in summer. As the first job, try to thin out the tangle of growth. The centre of the tree needs to be airy. Curving, low hanging branches, if not required for their picturesque effect, are best shortened to an upright stem. Crossing stems should be removed. Those which hang so low that the lawn mower (human!) is in peril should be removed entirely. Generally speaking, try to prune so that no branch is less than a yard above the one below it and none are nearer to each other than 2 feet.

Be warned! If you have a tree which is a tangle of barren branches this is quite likely to be the result of bad pruning in which someone has cut back the young growth annually with no plan and no purpose other than believing that this was what pruning really is and that it had to be done. If you are not sure how to cope call in the expert. Every county has a horticultural advisory officer who will advise gardeners.

Plums, being grafted, are inclined to produce suckers from their stocks. Obviously, these should not be allowed to grow. Instead they must be removed right down to the root from which they grow. This operation entails some digging.

Wall climbers and trained plants often offer problems and need patience and understanding to bring them under control. Pruning of climbers should always be done very carefully for it is so easy to remove the growth on which the current year's flowers would have been borne. It is not good to try to tidy a flowering wall plant by clipping it with shears in spring or winter for this reason, although it is quite all right to clip ivy, Virginia creeper and other self-clinging climbers.

Generally, the same rule applies to climbers and so-called climbers as to other shrubs; cut one or two important stems instead of taking tiny pieces from all over. You can usually see which is the oldest and least vigorous branch just as it is easy to see which branches are overcrowded. On a wall, a plant cannot so naturally grow its own way to sunlight. It is up to the gardener to space the stems so that each has its own share.

It may be that the climber has become loosened from its supports and it is these which need renewing more than the plant itself. In this case ask yourself if it is wise to go back to the original means of support or whether it would not be better to employ some more modern and/or improved means. There is a variety of methods to choose from.

You may not be well acquainted with the climber in question so a general rule may be helpful. Like shrubs, they flower either on the current season's growth, the new wood, and are generally in bloom from summer to autumn, or, they flower on the previous year's growth, the old wood, and are generally in bloom from early spring until early summer.

Those that flower early in the year on the previous summer's growth should be pruned immediately after flowering. Others should be pruned at such a time as to give the longest season for growth preparatory to flowering. If you are not sure what climber you have, wait to see it flower and get it identified. If your climber is grown only for its leaf coverage and not for bloom, it may be pruned back as follows: if deciduous any time from late October until March, if evergreen from late February to early April.

Climbers which present a tangle of matted thin growth such as clematis, jasmine, honeysuckle, polygonum, can be drastically cut right back and given a chance to begin anew. But it would be unwise to do this to such a lovely and long-lived climber as wisteria or grape vine. The latter needs careful pruning and if you can, it is wise to call in an expert.

Wisterias produce many shoots each year. If these are not required to grow on to occupy wall space they should be cut back, in August, to about 12 inches, making the cut directly above a leaf; remember that the flowers are only produced at the base of the shoots. If necessary, prune again in winter, shortening side growths to two growth buds. This climber need not be pruned except if it is growing in a restricted area where it must be kept within bounds. If you have to remove a large portion cut it right back to a main stem.

Hedges in old gardens often need attention, spreading in width and encroaching on the garden. You can cut them back quite drastically without killing them. It is best to be quite bold and prune one side of the hedge one year, taking the branches back to the centre stems, and the other side the next. Treat the side which gets most sun first. You may be surprised to see how quickly the new growth springs from every part of the old branches. Once this new growth gets going, it can feed the plants while the other side is cut back the same way.

If there are holes in the hedge, take stems from either side and tie them together across the gap. If the gap occurs at the base of the hedge, it is sometimes possible to layer a stem or two, thus filling the space.

Old hedges need feeding. Liberally mulch the soil over the roots with animal manure, compost or any good organic food.

For the neglected garden in general, having decided what to keep in its present home, decide what must be moved. Most plants, however mature, can be moved if the season and the weather are right. But move them quickly. Prepare their new homes before you lift them. Remember, too that any plant uprooted from its anchorage is suffering a drastic operation, and its growth and development will be checked for a year or two. Be sure that the soil is in good heart so that the plant feeds well.

Often in old gardens, soil becomes starved. The soil itself is of good texture (indeed often these wasted soils are very easy indeed to work) but its riches have been drawn from it by successive generations of plants and its vitality must be restored. Humus is the only ingredient that will restore maximum growing powers to any soil. (See chapter on Soil.)

One indication that all is not well with the soil in your garden is the state of the lawn. Lawns need fresh air below, near the roots. The only way you can get it there is to go all over the surface, plunging a digging fork in and rocking it a little to open up the holes made by the tines. Alternatively, you can use a spiker; there are several examples on the market, specially designed for the job. If you have reason to believe that the soil below the lawn is not well drained (an indication of this is the tendency for water to hang about) scatter coarse sand over the spiked area and brush the surface with a hard broom so that the sand filters down into the holes. This will help aerate the soil below. Moss is usually a sign that the soil is either poor or badly drained – or both. It can also be caused by cutting the grass too closely too often.

Moss can be killed by one of the special compounds designed for the task. Mere raking too often spreads the spores and leads to more trouble. You can make your own moss killer by applying sulphate of iron at a rate of about $\frac{1}{4}$ ounce per square yard. As this is such a small quantity it will be easier to mix the sulphate of iron with sand and spread this over the mossy places.

Very rough grass is better scythed at first, either by hand with an old-fashioned scythe or with a motor scythe. If it is not really a very large patch get down on your knees, and cut it with the shears or an old-fashioned sickle and stick. You need not get it very short to begin with. Rake all mowings away and use them for mulching or compost.

I really can assure you that the more you cut rough grass the better it becomes.

While I personally deplore an over-tidy garden, I believe that constantly trimmed lawn edges make a lawn look well groomed. Often an old lawn has ragged edges. These can be righted without a great deal of trouble. Take a garden line, or, alternatively, use the edge of a board and trim first with an edge cutter or a spade, cutting right through the turf. After this, keep the fringe of new grass which constantly grows trimmed with the edging shears and avoid cutting into the soil or your lawn will become smaller and your borders wider. You will not need a line after the first trim.

If the edges of the lawn are ragged or worn away in some places and you do not wish to cut the edge to make the lawn smaller, you can smarten them by neatly removing a turf from the ragged portion and then turning it so that the good straight inside edge now becomes the outside edge. The ragged piece, now inwards, can be patched by filling it with a mixture of good sifted soil and grass seed. Mix

some ready for patching using a large bucket of good fine soil and a ¼ pound of good grass seed.

A very small garden might be better used as a mere root-hold for some striking plant to grow on the house or the dividing wall or fence, some plant to boast of, an unusual climber, a wonderful rose or a passion flower. This could be balanced by another plant of architectural beauty in a pot, a yucca perhaps or some fascinating example of bonsai, which today are more easily found and cheaper than they used to be.

Too often a tiny garden is divided into four by little cross paths which usually have the effect of making the garden and the house look even smaller than they are. Try converting the garden by making a path from corner to corner instead. You will find this much easier to maintain. If you like to experiment a little further and if you have the room, make this a diagonal curve, a lazy S, and you will find it even more attractive. You can lessen your work by making one side of the path a place where trees and shrubs grow and the other side a site for more temporary plants, perhaps flowers in the foreground and vegetables at the back.

A rectangular lawn surrounded by rectangular strips makes for formal and consequently demanding gardening. Change the lawn shape to an oval or a circle. The beds will then vary in depth. Shrubs can be planted in the wider areas for permanent display. Perennials can be grown in the narrower sections but you can also use these for block plantings according to season. In this way, only part of the border will need annual attention.

If you begin with a grassed area and intend cutting borders into this, bamboos stuck in the ground will help you 'draw' the plans. Some gardeners use the hose laid out on the ground to define a shape. Before you cut in the grass, take the mower along the outline and see that it takes the curves easily and alter the outline where necessary. Remember that while wavy-edged borders look lovely they must not be so scalloped that they are fussy or difficult to maintain.

Paths should be serviceable and safe as well as decorative. See the section on Paving for more details. In the meantime, by altering the present paths you may be able to give the garden a new look.

Choosing the right plants can make a great deal of difference to the scene. If you have a long, narrow garden, try planting round cushiony plants rather than tall spiky ones or clip any suitable existing ones into shape.

Many a gardener taking over a neglected plot is charmed to find a pool, overgrown and neglected,

Trimming the lawn edge with a sharp edging tool and a plank. Badly worn edges are remedied by turning the turf the other way round and seeding the bare patch perhaps, but nevertheless a garden pool. Yet when he comes to clear it and fill it with water he finds that the concrete is cracked and broken and that it will not hold water. He tries to patch it, but nothing seems to make it completely watertight, so in the end he breaks up the concrete in disgust and fills in the depression.

Obviously, there are degrees of damage and dilapidation. Where the pool is badly broken, no amount of make do and mend will ever bring it back into a good state. But bear in mind always with a pool of any kind that the major part of the constructional work has already been done – the actual digging and carting away of excavated soil – so it is always worth trying to take advantage of this earlier work.

Where the concrete of the pool is merely cracked in places, it is possible to bring it back into good condition by painting *all* the surface with a special sealing compound such as Aquaseal. This is a bituminous material, thick and sticky but not unlike paint. If several layers are given to the concrete, special attention being given to the more obvious cracks, then the entire surface will be sealed and the pool will hold water again. Be very thorough about this and do not imagine that because you cannot see a crack none exists. Far better to go over places which are already waterproof than to neglect some

parts, only to find that the water must be drained out again and the whole pool be given another coat of the sealing compound.

On the other hand, if the pool is obviously in very bad condition, some pieces of concrete having fallen out or broken away, do not despair. It is still worth the effort of rehabilitation. First coat the broken places with a special adhesive for concrete and then fill in with fresh cement. Then coat the whole pool with a bituminous compound and, while this is still wet, patch the worst areas with plastic sheeting. Use a patch considerably larger than the hole and smooth the sheeting evenly over the area. Finally, paint again with at least two coats over the entire area. The bituminous compound may be obtained in several colours, usually black, blue or stone.

But sometimes the concrete pool will be so damaged and broken that it is past all repair. Nevertheless, the hole exists, so try to make use of this. Carefully break up and remove all the existing concrete, leaving the entire hole with a mere soil lining. If the soil is stony or if there are projecting roots, line the base and sides with fine sand or peat. Then lay over the whole of the area a sheet of heavy duty plastic lining material specially made for pools and make the pool just as you would a new one.

Planning the new garden

Every garden is a challenge in one way or another but sometimes a new garden whether left by the builders or by its ex-owner is almost a threat! But take heart! Many of the prettiest and most entertaining gardens I know have been made by people who knew nothing or little about gardening when they began.

Three truisms about planning a small garden might bear repeating: 1, plan carefully before you begin; 2, make use of and exploit every inch of space, and 3, select your plants with great care.

To assess what features are necessary, let your eyes go beyond the boundaries of your garden. If there is a lovely tree far away, 'steal' it. Plant your own trees in front of it so that the in-between scene (if this is not attractive) is hidden and the tree appears

to be an extension of your own plants and your garden. If there are many trees in the distance, or even in neighbouring gardens, imagine your garden against the backcloth made by them and group your plants accordingly. This way your garden will appear bigger.

The owner of a new plot filled with nothing but builder's rubble thinks first of his lawn, then of trees and shrubs. Once the grass is down, the garden begins to look established. Then the plot must be furnished. It is possible, even in this country where the techniques of moving large trees are seldom practised, to obtain first-class *mature* examples of many decorative trees and shrubs. Some firms issue a special list of large specimen trees and shrubs for immediate effect which create the impression of an apparently mature garden from the emptiest meadowland. Prices however, are necessarily comparatively high for large trees, for they require techniques in both growing and moving.

Most of us are faced, therefore, with the alternative of planning our garden by looking ahead ten years or more to imagine the final effects we hope to achieve. Small trees and shrubs are astonishingly inexpensive and when bought from a reputable nurseryman almost foolproof. Except for certain quick-growing varieties these will develop little in the first year or two of their newly planted life. After this, however, when reasonably well established, they will romp away, accelerating in the speed of their growth until they become no longer seedlings but sturdy young plants that play a vital part in the landscaping of the garden. Meanwhile the imaginative gardener can fill the space with quick-growing annuals that can furnish the garden with leafy plants.

Let us consider the really new garden, the uncultivated building site – a pathetic wilderness of weeds and builder's rubble, often without protection or privacy, its soil nothing more than a churned-up mixture of baked clay and half bricks! What is one to do with it?

Should one first defend it with fences or hedges, decorate it with trees and shrubs, cover it with a carpet of green turf, utilise it for a children's playground or cultivate it for fruit and vegetables? Before we begin to scheme, let us ask ourselves what a garden should provide.

Most of us feel that it should make and be a lovely setting for the home and provide an extension of our living room. Indoors, the first thing you have to do is sweep and scrub the floors. In the garden, you must first clear the ground and remove the debris. This is the worst job of all, but you should not try to rush it. Do not, for instance be in a hurry to get rid of broken bricks and other rubble. Stack it in a heap. You may want it later as a foundation for paths or perhaps to drain a lawn. If the soil is naturally stony, save the stones. Grade them as you gather them into drainage, wall or path-surface size. Do not bother to try to pick up small stones. These help aerate the soil.

Once the site is cleared, you must dig and dig. This is probably better done with a fork rather than a spade, which is liable to chop through the taprooted weeds like dandelions, thus propagating them. The fork will loosen the long roots and enable you to remove them. Always keep a container handy for these roots, and get rid of them by burning as soon as possible. If the tops are leafy, twist off this vegetation and use it on the compost heap which you ought to

get going as soon as possible. If your soil is very light or sandy, you may find that only a spade is suitable for digging.

It is sometimes possible to hire a rotary digger. This will turn the ground over and also help to level it quite efficiently, but once done you should take special care to rake up all weeds, roots and fibrous matter.

Often the worst trouble in a new garden is mud, particularly if the builders have recently left. So it is to everyone's advantage to cover the ground as quickly as possible. You may be able to anticipate bigger jobs this way, for example, if you have planned where patio, paved paths or drives are going, then have a load of gravel delivered and get these areas covered.

A grassed area makes a garden look neater immediately. It keeps down the mud brought into the house, gives the children somewhere to play, keeps the soil in good heart until you are ready to make beds and borders, gives you valuable humus in the form of grass cuttings.

If there is grass already – and on building sites old meadow often exists – it can be mown for immediate tidiness. Most likely it can become a good lawn. Remember that grass is a good clean covering, and is well worth keeping, even if it covers a larger area than you actually want as lawn. Even if you plan to get going on beds and borders fairly soon, you will find it an advantage to get the grass cut as soon as possible for you can cut into the short turf with a spade much more easily than you will be able to into the hussocks of uncut grass. Another advantage is that once the lawn is down big jobs, such as planning a new border, can be shelved to a convenient planting time.

Never take up grass roots or turves to burn (the pestilent couch grass is an exception). Rotted grass roots and turves make highly valued loam.

The turves you cut away when you design the borders need only be skimmed off the surface. First cut through with a spade, making a rough square, then slide the spade along under the turf as though it were a fish slice. You can then stack the turves grass side downwards. When they have rotted, they can be put back on the garden as good fibrous loam. You can also use turves stacked this way as banks or low dividing walls. Pull out any tap roots of weeds.

Should you wish, you can let the turf stay and dig right through it, taking a slice of grass with every spadeful. In this case, see that you turn each spadeful so that the grass lies at the bottom and becomes well covered. It will then rot.

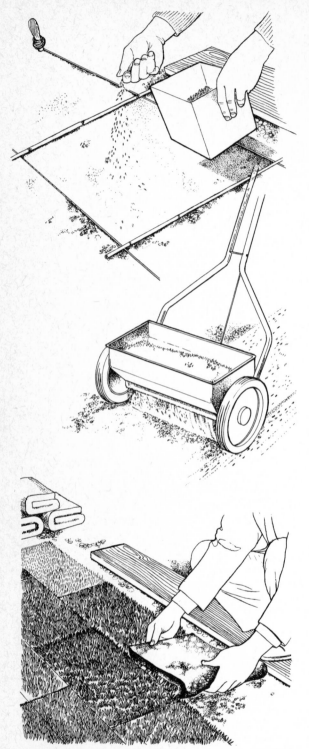

If you have been able to clear your site or the area intended for the lawn without much trouble, you would be wise to get it covered as early in your garden scheme as possible. Get the surface for the new lawn as level as you can. If you are a perfectionist use pegs, string and a spirit level. Otherwise, rake with a board or garden line to guide you. If your garden slopes, it may be best to break it up into a series of level terraces with retaining walls like steps between them. If you have children, you can give them a lower terrace for playing while you make the higher ones pretty for yourself.

Remember that if the garden slopes away from the house you will not see much of it from your windows. Levelling this would be a major task, but you could make a wall or rock garden at the bottom and push it up. If you decide to keep the slope, rake across, not downwards, to prevent soil and later seed from washing away.

You can use seed or turves (regular pieces of grass taken from a field) for your lawn. Turves are convenient because they can be laid at any time except in frosty weather. Grass seed will often germinate at any time, but is best sown in September or March.

Most good seedsmen make up special lawn seed mixtures to suit soils (clay or sand), situations (sun or shade) and use (heavy or light). Be sure to specify your requirements when you order. Where the children will play on the lawn it is best to use a hard-wearing mixture which includes some rye grass, although this will require regular mowing. Average prices here are about 50 to 60p a pound. Finer mixtures without rye grass need less cutting but won't take such tough usage. These can cost 70 to 80p a pound for the very finest. All prices are rising. One pound of seed will cover an area of roughly 10 square yards. As I have already stressed many times, good drainage is essential.

Poor soils should always be enriched so that the grass is constantly nourished. Lichen and mosses can be a nuisance on a poor soil. You can use any good lawn fertiliser or bonemeal. Alternatively, you can make your own fertiliser by mixing 1 ounce of bonemeal, 1 ounce of superphosphate, $\frac{1}{2}$ ounce of sulphate of ammonia and $\frac{1}{4}$ ounce of sulphate of potash to every square yard. Rake this in a week before you sow the grass or lay the turves.

Lawns can be sown during the summer months but they need care and watering in a drought. After the first preparatory digging in spring and autumn, leave the soil in clods as you work (see section on Soil). Keep your eyes open for any weeds you may have overlooked. After two or three weeks, longer if

It is important to sow grass seed accurately and evenly either by dividing the plot into square yards or with a wheeled spreader. Alternatively a lawn can be made from turves possible, level the site, first breaking down the soil into finer particles with the digging fork and then raking to make a fine tilth suitable for seeds. Make sure that the surface is level.

If no soil sticks to your shoes, then the soil is dry and right for seed sowing. Either tread the whole surface (with flat shoes) or give it a *light* rolling to compact it. This will give the grass a firm root hold. Rake it lightly once more, just scratching the surface soil, so that it is ready to receive the seed.

This needs to be applied at the rate of $1\frac{1}{2}$ ounces a square yard and it is important to sow evenly. Some people divide the whole area to be sown into yard squares, marking them out with string or thick white thread, attached to pegs set at yard intervals at the lawn edges, and although this may seem extra work, it really is worthwhile. It is also worthwhile weighing and measuring $1\frac{1}{2}$ ounces – you may have a cup or some kitchen measure which will just hold this amount exactly, then all you have to do is to dip into the bag for each square yard. Wheeled spreaders are available which release measured amounts of seed. These give the more accurate results. You can frequently borrow one from your seedsman or garden centre.

Sow half the measureful in the marked-out square, shaking it lightly first from side to side, and then sow the other half the other way round from the top of the square to the base. This way the seed will be spread evenly over the whole area. You can use a flour sifter or a pierced tin or a jar with a pierced lid as a seed shaker. Have ready some fine sifted soil and cast this lightly over the seeded patch just to cover and weigh down the seeds.

If you keep the pegs in place, you can use them to stretch cotton criss-cross over the seeded area just above ground level to keep birds away. Seed may be treated with bird repellent – most seed is – but this will not stop the birds from having a taste before they are repelled, nor from using the nice fine soil as a dust bath. It really does not matter what colour the thread or cotton is, you want only to deter the birds not to trick them.

Grass seed usually germinates between 10 and 20 days after sowing, depending on the weather. Keep off the grass until the young leaves, or blades, are 2 inches high. At this point it may be mown carefully. Use a machine with a roller attached, rather than one with side wheels which will cut into the soil. If your machine is old, be sure to have the blades sharpened and set or the tiny plants will be pulled out of the soil. The mower blades need to be set so that they just tip the grass. Mow this way, just tipping the grass, once a week for a month. After this, gradually lower the blades.

If there is a drought be sure to water the young grass seedlings gently and thoroughly with a fine rose or a hose sprinkler system and give *plenty*. Sprinkling the surface will do more harm than good.

Weed seedlings may also appear with the grass. Some will disappear with mowing, others will be more persistent but wait a year before using a 'selective' weedkiller. These kill broad-leaved plants but not grasses, so take the greatest care not to let any spray fall on the borders. One or two preparations exist especially for newly sown lawns. Make quite sure before you use them. Selective weedkillers can be in liquid or lawn sand form.

The site for a turf lawn must always be prepared in exactly the same way as for sowing seed. Usually turves are cut in strips 3 feet by 1 foot and rolled like a swiss roll! But sometimes they are cut a foot square. The best turves are fairly uniform in thickness. Cheaper ones may not be so, and this complicates the job of laying them. It is worthwhile trimming them before laying instead of trying to adjust the level of the soil while you are laying them. To do this, make a frame, a box with one end missing, almost the same size as the turves but with a little to spare to make it easier to put them in and pull them out. The sides of the box should be the required thickness of the turves and any which are too thick can then be slid into the box grass-side downwards. Any surplus soil which juts above the box can then be sliced off with an old knife. Any that are too thin should be set aside or marked and when these are laid a little extra soil can be placed under them.

When the turves are delivered, have them stacked carefully in a place near the site of the lawn to avoid unnecessary handling. When you are ready, lay the turves on the prepared surface taking care that they all go one way, their side edges in line. Pack them as close to each other as you can. It is best to start at the lawn edges so that every fresh row of turves goes down on untrodden soil. You can walk on the turves themselves but, as they may become rather knocked about, it is better if you can place a board or plank over the area of soil where you will be working as you lay the next row of turves. This will spread your weight and prevent the soil from becoming consolidated.

Use the plank as a walk from the pile of turves across the laid turves. The joints of the second row of turves should come between those of the first row, rather as bricks do in a wall. Move the plank along as you work. Put aside any damaged turves and use these at the centre. Use good ones for the sides. If you notice any perennial weed roots when you are laying the turf, it is usually quite easy to prise them out.

When all the lawn is laid, beat the turves down with the back of the spade. This will compact them and help to push the joints together. Take some sifted soil or fine peat and scatter it over the turves. If you care to mix in a little grass seed this will help bind the turves even more quickly. Then brush the grass lightly all over, first from side to side and then from top to base. This will help fill up the joints. Water the soil thoroughly. You need not worry that you will wash away the seed as you would for a seeded lawn, but you must let the water get down right through the grass to the roots.

Wait at least two weeks before attempting to cut the grass and when you do, set the mower blades high for the first month. Adjust any difference in levels which become apparent when you first mow. You can use selective weedkillers after a month.

The blades of your mowing machine should be set at the correct height. If you have fine grass which you mow constantly set the blades just below a half inch, never lower than three-eighths. For stronger growing grass, blades should be set at half an inch. Mow in a different direction at each mowing so that if you mow the length of the lawn at one time, mow from the sides next time and diagonally after that. Do not roll often but a rolling in spring will compact the soil. Many people never roll the lawn at all. In spring (and before rolling) if you intend to do this, rake the lawn surface to remove leaves and other debris. Rake well using a special fan-shaped wire rake which will comb out creeping weeds, moss and old grass and so help to aerate the growing grass. This will also help to keep all kinds of fungus pests at bay.

Spiking or puncturing the lawn surface with a digging fork or a special spiked roller is also a good means of aerating the soil and improving drainage. In April, topdress the lawn by scattering fertiliser evenly over the surface. There are several good proprietary brands.

The pattern of your lawn can do much to distinguish your rectangular plot from others. An oddly shaped piece of land can be balanced by making a good central lawn of definite pattern.

It might be necessary to design the grass in relation to the house, extending the line down the centre. Of course the lawn need not be square or rectangular, but once you get it properly balanced you will find that definite borders can be made around it. Oddly shaped pieces left over can be used to hold specific sections such as a cutting patch, a fruit bed or a vegetable garden. Paths around them or to them can be screened, thus giving the impression that more lies beyond.

If the plot (taking the direction from the house) is long, make the lawn wide or circular. If it is too wide, make a diamond- or cameo-shaped lawn, running away from the house.

A round, heart-shaped, diamond-, cameo- or even rose-shaped lawn with scalloped edges may often look better than a rectangle, but make sure that the mower can easily negotiate the curving edges. A tiny garden may look prettier if the lawn is turned into a wide 'path' with flower borders on each side.

Remember that the area near any sunny wall or fence is valuable, so do not spoil it by placing the path next to it.

If you are going to grow a shrub or tree that needs to be savoured for its scent or admired closely for the beauty of its flowers do not plant it way back but set it near the path, unless it is a very thorny one.

Do not restrict your planting or planning to establishing all tall plants at the sides of the garden coming down the scale to the dwarfs in front. Break up the contours so that a low shrub is sometimes hidden from the house behind a taller one for you to find with new pleasure every time you walk down the garden.

If you move house in autumn, winter or early spring you can safely transplant well-grown shrubs and even small trees. But make sure first that you are legally entitled to take garden plants with you when you move. As soon as you know when you are going to move, begin by making a cut round the roots of the plant. You need to go in a circle some distance from the stem of the plant and the older it is the further out you will need to cut the soil. The smallest distance is 1 foot. Make a small trench around the base of the tree. The more you can do the better, but remember that a tree will be very heavy.

Fill your circular trench with moist peat to encourage fibrous roots to grow. Every week or so, thrust the spade in again if you think the main roots are not properly cut. When the weather is dry, water the peat in the trench. When the time comes to move the tree, really soak the peat two days before lifting. Have ready a sack or a sheet of strong polythene spread out on the ground and cut the roots under the tree. Dig out the trench so that you can level a spade, and push it under the roots to cut through them so that you can make what we call a 'root ball'.

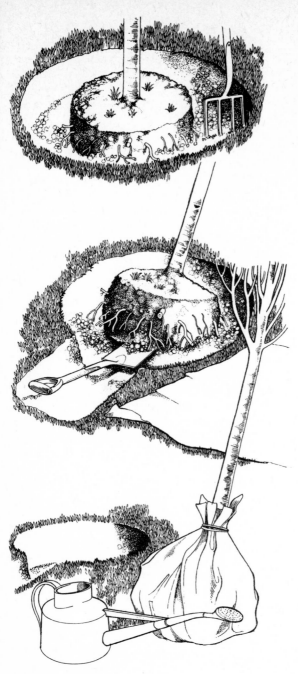

Lifting and balling an established tree

I find it is best if two of you do this job, one on each side of the tree. When the root ball is properly severed, lift it immediately into the sack and quickly cover the roots. Spray the foliage with a watering-can and if the plant is to hang about for any length of time keep the leaves well watered. A fairly short-lived plastic coating material applied as an aerosol spray and merely known as S600, can be employed to coat the foliage of a tree or shrub that is to be moved and

so considerably reduce transpiration. It is colourless and disappears after a few weeks in normal weathering.

When you are planting, make a hole at least 4 feet in diameter, put your plant in the centre of it on soil which has been enriched, taking care that you re-plant it at the same level. You don't want the root ball above or below the present soil level.

Town gardens often present special problems. A small town garden is usually a shady garden, so unless you are certain that the position chosen is open to the sun, select from the wide range of plants suitable for shady positions, which include aucuba, camellia, cornus, euonymus, hypericum, mahonia, olearia, skimmia and symphoricarpos.

Remember that every inch of soil is precious. Never let a wasteful weed rob the soil of nourishment or moisture. So use ground cover plants such as bergenia, daboecia, erica, euonymus, hypericum and pachysandra.

It is easy to get a riot of colour in summer, but think also of the darker months. Trees and shrubs that flower in winter include *Chimonanthus praecox*, *Daphne mezereum*, some of the ericas, forsythia, *Garrya elliptica*, *Jasminum nudiflorum*, several mahonias, *Prunus davidiana*, *Lonicera fragrantissima*, *Prunus subhirtella autumnalis* and *Viburnum fragrans*.

Many town gardens, apart from getting little light through the smoky atmosphere, also suffer by deposits of toxic minerals such as sulphur. Some plants just cannot take it for long and need replacing frequently. These are tougher: *Acer platanoides*, berberis, betula, *Buddleia davidii*, catalpa, chaenomeles, cornus, cotoneaster, crataegus, *Daphne mezereum*, euonymus, forsythia, holly, ivy, jasmine, laburnum, laurel, *Mahonia aquifolium*, malus, prunus, pyracantha, ribes, senecio, symphoricarpos, sorbus, syringa, veronica and viburnum.

It is all very well deciding what kind of a garden you would like and making pretty plans on paper, but your dreams have eventually to be translated into reality and your plans into actual seeds, plants, bricks, paving stones and concrete. And if you have never had to think along these lines before it is difficult to know what materials are available, where they can be obtained and what quantities you will require for your special purposes.

So the following information is severely practical. Seeds are easy enough to buy in so many places and plants can either be obtained from local nurseries or garden shops or by mail from one of the many national nurseries. Your local builder or builders' merchant will be able to supply such materials as bricks, gravel and paving stones. He will also advise you on quantities and methods of using the materials you buy from him. Alternatively, some of the larger garden centres or garden sundriesmen will be able to supply you with virtually everything you can possibly need.

But first it is always well to know the surface area of your whole garden, as well as the area of special places such as beds, borders, pools and terraces. For a regular shaped plot, a square or a rectangle, it is easy enough to measure down the garden and then across and multiply these two figures together. This will give you the surface area in square feet or yards, depending on which you use. But what about an irregular shape? Here measure the longest part and shortest part, add these lengths together and divide by two. Now measure the widest and narrowest parts, add together and divide by two. Multiply together the two answers you get and there you are again with your result in square feet or yards.

To measure a circle, multiply the radius (the distance from the exact centre to the side) by itself and multiply your result by $3\frac{1}{7}$th. For example, if the radius is 5 feet, then $5 \times 5 \times 3\frac{1}{7}$th equals 78 square feet, or near enough. And to find the number of gallons of water in a circular pool carry out the calculation just shown, multiply your answer (78) by the depth of the pool (say 2 feet, equals 156) and then multiply this result by $6\frac{1}{4}$ (equals 975). In other words, then, a pool with a diameter (right the way across or twice the radius) of 10 feet and 2 feet deep, will need very nearly 1,000 gallons of water to fill it to the top.

And the number of gallons in a rectangular pool is even easier to find. Just multiply the length by the width by the depth in feet and multiply this result by $6\frac{1}{4}$. (The $6\frac{1}{4}$, by the way, is merely the number of gallons in a cubic foot.)

If you are going to have fish in your pool you must have the right number. If there are too few the water will get cloudy and if there are too many there will not be sufficient air for them and some will die. So allow 1 inch of fish body length (excluding the tail) to 4 gallons of water, or, if you like, 4 inches of body length to 1 square foot of water surface area.

It is well to remember, though, that your fish will grow and may multiply, so always allow a small margin for this. If you get too many baby fish for your pool, let them grow until they are at least 2 inches long before you get them out carefully with a net and give them to neighbours.

Knowing your areas you can order your materials.

Sand or gravel usually comes by the 'load' or by the ton. A load is one cubic yard (27 cubic feet). This will cover roughly 15 to 17 square yards at about 2 to 3 inches deep. A ton is slightly less, containing about 20 cubic feet, which will cover about 10 to 12 square yards to the same depth.

Paving stone is of two types. There are the regular slabs of various sizes and in several pastel colours. It is easy enough to work out how many of these you will require. Irregular shapes, such as you would use for crazy paving, usually come by the ton, which contains about 13 to 14 cubic feet. This will cover from 8 to 16 square yards, depending on thickness and method of laying. Most paving is $1\frac{1}{2}$ to 2 inches thick.

You can make your own paving stones from concrete but as a rule you will find you save very little by doing so. You can, however, make special shapes and colours if you care to do it yourself. Never make them too large; they are very heavy.

If you want to make a good path you can calculate your requirements from this specimen. A path 20 feet long and 3 feet wide will require roughly: 10 to 15 hundredweights ($\frac{1}{4}$ to $\frac{1}{2}$ yard) of gravel 2 to 3 inches deep; 12 hundredweights of York paving slabs; 16 hundredweights of crazy paving 2 inches thick; 215 bricks laid flat. Or if you wish to lay concrete for this path you will need 9 hundredweights of gravel or aggregate, 3 hundredweights of sand and 3 hundredweights of cement to make the path 2 inches thick.

Most fencing today comes in ready-made panels of certain standard sizes, usually about 6 feet wide and varying in height from about 3 feet to about 6 feet. If you wish to make your own fences, you will have to decide on the type and quantity of timber you will require, but remember that a 'square' of timber contains 100 square feet.

Walling can consist of stone, bricks or concrete slabs of different shapes and kinds. There is a wide choice and you have an opportunity here to break away from the ordinary and make some pretty patterns. Some of the comparatively new kinds of walling come in blocks with various holes and patterns in them. They are usually called 'screen walling'. This gives a lighter effect, can be very attractive, and lets in some light and air.

To see what kinds of walling are available, and in fact to obtain all kinds of information about the use of concrete in the garden – paving, walling, pools, pergolas – you can get excellent free leaflets from the Cement and Concrete Association, 52 Grosvenor Gardens, London S.W.1.

List of plants for specified conditions

E – EVERGREEN
D – DECIDUOUS
C – CLIPPED (This indicates plants which can receive formal clipping rather than mere trimming)
U – UNCLIPPED
T – TALL (more than 3 feet)
S – SHORT (less than 3 feet)
F – FLOWERING
B – BERRYING OR FRUITING

Berberis, E and D, U, T, and S, F and B
Buxus (Box), E, C, S
Carpinus (Hornbeam), D (but holds leaves during winter) S, C
Chaenomeles (Japonica), D, U, T, F
Chamaecyparis, E, C and U, T
Cornus (Dogwood), D, U, T, F and B
Cotoneaster, E, and D, C and U, T and S, F and B
Crataegus (Thorn, Quick or May), D, C, T, F and B
Cupressocyparis, E, C, T
Cupressus, E, C or U, T
Deutzia, D, U, S, F
Erica (Heather), E, C or U, S, F
Escallonia, D, U, T, F
Fagus (Beech), D (but holds leaves in winter) C, T
Forsythia, D, U, T, F
Fuchsia, D, U, T, F
Hebe (Veronica), E, U, S, F
Hippophae (Sea Buckthorn), D, U, T, B
Ilex (Holly), E, C or U, T or S, B
Kerria, D, U, S, F
Lavandula (Lavender), E, C or U, S, F
Ligustrum (Privet), E, C, T or S
Lonicera, E, C, T or S
Myrtus (Myrtle), E, U, S, F and B
Olearia, E, U, S, F
Osmarea, E, U, T or S, F
Philadelphus, D, U, T or S, F
Pittosporum, E, U, T
Potentilla, D, U, S, F
Prunus (several), D, C or U, T or S, F and/or B
Pyracantha, E, U, T or S, F and B
Ribes, D, C or U, T, F
Rosa (Rose, several), D, U, T or S, F and B
Rosemarinus (Rosemary), E, C or U, T or S, F
Santolina, E, U, S, F
Spiraea, D, U, T or S, F

Symphoricarpos (Snowberry), D, C or U, T, B
Syringa (Lilac), D, C or U, T, F
Taxus (Yew), E, C, T
Thuya, E, C or U, T
Viburnum, E, U, T, F and B
Weigela (Diervilla), D, U, T, F
Note: some of the berrying plants (e.g. Ilex and Hippophae) require male and female plants to produce their fruits.

Herbaceous and Bulbous Plants for Shade

Aconitum
Alchemilla
Anemone
Aquilegia
Bergenia
Campanula
Convallaria
    (Lily-of-the-valley)
Gentiana
Geranium (Cranesbill)
Helleborus
Hosta
Hypericum
Meconopsis
Polygonum
Primula
Pulmonaria
Ramonda
Saxifraga
Tradescantia
Tropaeolum
Viola

Weed-suppressing Ground Cover Plants

Clear ground thoroughly before planting at 1- to 3-foot intervals. It may take a few seasons before the soil is completely covered.

Cotoneaster conspicuus
    decorus
C. horizontalis
C. microphyllus
Cytisus beanii
C. kewensis
C. purpureus incarnatus
Daboecia
Erica
Euonymus radicans
Genista hispanica
Hedysarum
Hypericum calycinum
H. moserianum
Juniperus (prostrate varieties)
Lavandula spica
Mahonia aquifolium
Pachysandra
Pernettya
Santolina
Sarcococca
Symphoricarpos
Viburnum davidii
Vinca major
V. minor

Climbing Plants for Walls

s.c. – self clinging. Remainder must be supported by trellis or wires
E. – evergreen
N.S.E.W. – North-, South-, East- or West-facing walls

Actinidia, s.w.
Ampelopsis, s.c., N.S.E.W.
Bignonia, s.w.
Clematis, s.w.
C. montana, N.S.E.W.
Coronilla, E., s.w.
Hedera, s.c., E., N.S.E.W.
Hydrangea petiolaris, s.c., N.S.E.W.
Jasminum, N.S.E.W.
Lonicera, N.S.E.W.
Passiflora, s.w.
Polygonum, N.S.E.W.
Rosa (climbing varieties), s.w.
Schizophragma, N.S.E.W.
Solanum, s.w.
Vitis, s.w.
Wisteria, s.w.

Shrubs for Shade

Acer (Maple)	Gaultheria
Andromeda	Hedera (Ivy)
Arundinaria	Hypericum
Aucuba	Juniperus
Azalea	Kerria
Berberis	Pachysandra
Buxus (Box)	Pyracantha
Camellia	Rhododendron
Chaenomeles (Japonica)	Ribes
Choisya	Ruscus
Cornus (Dogwood)	Sambucus
Cotoneaster	Skimmia
Daphne	Viburnum
Euonymus	Vinca (Periwinkle)
Garrya	

Trees and Shrubs for Alkaline (Limy) Soils

Acer campestre	Laburnum
Berberis	Ligustrum
Buxus	Juniperus
Cistus	Philadelphus
Clematis	Prunus
Cornus	Rhus
Cotoneaster	Sorbus
Crataegus	Symphoricarpos
Erica carnea	Syringa
Euonymus	Taxus
Fagus	Viburnum
Fraxinus	

Trees and Shrubs for Acid Soils

Abies	Eucryphia
Acer palmatum	Fothergilla
Amelanchier	Gaultheria
Andromeda	Hamamelis
Arundinaria	Hydrangea
Azalea	Ilex
Betula	Kalmia
Camellia	Magnolia
Chamaecyparis	Parrotia
Cupressus	Picea
Cytisus	Pinus
Daboecia	Rhododendron
Enkianthus	Tsuga
Erica	

Glossary

Acid Soils are termed acid, neutral or alkaline. Acidity and alkalinity can be measured. One talks of the pH of a soil, pH7 is neutral. Above this it is alkaline or limy, below, acid. (See section on Soil.)

Aerial Not all roots are below the soil. Some appear on the stems of plants, such as ivy, and assist them to climb or to feed from the moist air.

Alpine Applied to garden plants this means almost any plant suitable for a rock garden. Usually, a a small plant which does not need deep cultivation.

American Blight or Woolly Aphis Usually appears on apple trees. Destroy by tar-oil spray, nicotine or methylated spirits.

Annual A plant that germinates, flowers and seeds within a year. Not all annuals take twelve months for their life cycle. Some flower and seed several times in a year.

Aphids Plant lice which suck juices from plants and often in doing so pass on virus diseases. Destroy and prevent by using insecticides either before or after these pests appear.

Aquatic In horticulture, any plant that grows in or from water.

Aroid Any plant which belongs to the arum family.

Bacteria One-celled, minute creatures extremely diverse, but divided roughly, horticulturally, into two groups, aerobic and anaerobic. Most of the first are beneficial but they cannot live without air. For this reason it is important to aerate the soil. Some bacteria can fix nitrogen from the air. This type live in the nodules seen on the roots of plants of the pea family.

Bedding Plants Any plant grown in a special display bed, usually applied to plants that are of a temporary nature.

Biennial Any plant whose life is spread over two years during which time it germinates, grows, flowers and seeds. Some perennials, for convenience, are treated as biennials; wallflowers and forget-me-nots are examples.

Big Bud A disorder caused by mites which live in the buds of currants, usually blackcurrants, and cause them to swell and become infected and useless. Spray in spring with lime sulphur. Pick buds off in winter and burn. Cut badly infected bushes to within a few inches of the ground – burn prunings.

Black Fly Any black aphid, most common on broad beans.

Black Spot A troublesome and serious rose disease most prevalent away from industrial areas. A fungus which attacks the foliage causing leaves to develop round, black spots. Burn infected leaves. Spray with colloidal copper.

Blanching A method of eliminating the indigestible dark green colouring from certain vegetables. Soil is drawn up round stems, over roots. Alternatively, light is excluded by some other means.

Blight Usually applied to aphids but also to any bad pest. Correctly applied to the fungus disease which affects potatoes. To prevent, spray early in June with Bordeaux mixture and again three or four weeks later.

Brassica The term applying to all members of the cabbage family. Kale, swede and Brussels sprouts are brassicas as well as cabbage and savoy.

Broccoli A brassica. There are several types of broccoli. Some produce large white heads (or cauliflowers) and are often called 'heading' broccoli. Others produce smaller shoots or sprouts, purple or green. Calabrese produces small green heads at first and smaller sprouts later.

Bulb A collection of swollen, fleshy leaves, which serve as food reservoirs. Really, a compact plant.

Canker A general name for a variety of fungal diseases. Reliable remedies are sold.

Capsid Bug Small insects; some beneficial, some harmful. Harmful types are aphid-like, white or green. They attack flower buds of apples in particular and cause deformed fruits. Destroy by spraying.

Clamp A heap of root vegetables, covered by clean

straw, sealed by earth beaten smooth. Used principally for potatoes but also for swedes, beetroots, carrots and dahlias.

Compost Confusedly, used in two ways, either to mean organic fertiliser made by composting vegetable refuse from the garden or alternatively, for soil mixtures of all kinds used for potting plants or seed sowing.

Cordon A naturally branching stem pruned and restricted to a single, double or sometimes, triple main stem.

Corm A storage organ, not unlike a bulb. The difference is that a corm is composed mainly of a thickened stem and is solid throughout.

Cotyledon A seed leaf. The majority of plants are divided into two groups. Monocotyledons have one seed leaf – grass is an example. Dicotyledons have two seed leaves – mustard and cress are examples.

Crown The upper part of the root and the area from which new growth starts. Sometimes used loosely to describe certain roots that are lifted for forcing.

Cutting Any portion of a plant which when cut or separated from it grows roots to become a new plant.

Damping off Various fungal diseases that mainly cause seedlings to decay, usually because they are over-crowded, suffocated or too damp.

Deciduous A plant which loses its leaves in winter. Some though, when young, retain the dead leaf until it is pushed off by the new bud swelling in the spring.

Drawn Tall, thin, weak and liable to collapse. Over-crowded plants and seedlings become drawn.

Drill A furrow made in the soil.

Earthing up The process of drawing soil above the crowns of plants, usually done with a hoe, either to anchor them (brassicas in winter); to blanch them (leeks or celery); or to prevent tubers being exposed to light, (potatoes).

Frame A structure made of wood, brick, cement, metals, turves or bales of straw, like a topless and bottomless box. As a cover a 'light' made of glass or plastic is used.

Fruit tree bands 'Fly-papers' which are placed round trunks and limbs of fruit trees, 3 feet above the ground, to trap insects, usually wingless, which damage crops and trees. The bands should remain on the trees until April.

Fungicide Any substance which will kill fungi. Reliable sprays are on sale everywhere. Bordeaux mixture, lime sulphur and others are quite safe. Copper sulphate mixture damages some foliage and often should only be used in winter.

Grease banding See Fruit tree bands.

Hardening off Accustoming plants to a cooler environment than that in which they were germinated and grown.

Heel The small strip of bark and wood retained on the base of a stem when it has been pulled away, usually downwards, from a main stem.

Heeling in Temporary planting, usually in a trench, where plants may be laid close together at an angle of 45 degrees, their roots covered with soil firmed by the foot.

Herb Technically, any plant which has soft or fibrous but not woody growth. The term is also used for any aromatic plant used in cooking.

Herbaceous border An area, usually backed by a fence, hedge or wall, given up to the cultivation of herbaceous plants.

Hot bed A warm area of soil laid on top of a heating medium, usually animal manure or electric heating cable, on which early crops of vegetables can be grown.

Humus Decayed organic material. Animal manure, leaves, grass, peat, kitchen refuse, seaweed, are all a source of humus. Chemical fertilisers are not.

Insecticide Any substance which will destroy insects.

Lateral A sideshoot. In fruit trees it will grow from a branch, from the single 'rod' or stem of a cordon and from the arms of an espalier.

Layer A shoot or stem encouraged to make roots while it is still attached to the parent plant. When rooted it should be severed and planted elsewhere.

Leader The main branch of a bush, the vertical extension of a cordon, the horizontal extension of an espalier.

Leafmould This term has two meanings. It is applied to the residue of year-old and older, stacked and rotted leaves – a rich source of humus. Beech and oak leaves make the best leafmould. It also refers to a leaf disease of tomatoes.

Lime Horticulturally, different forms of calcium. For example ground chalk, limestone, hydrated lime and slaked lime. A plant food, although some plants appear to do without it. A corrective for over-acid and too-clayey soils.

Loam Rotted turf. Ideally a perfectly balanced mixture of clay, humus and sand, but a term often used to describe different kinds of soil.

Mulch A covering for the soil; technically, a top-dressing applied fairly heavily.

Offsets Young plants or bulbs produced at the base or alongside another plant and easily detached.

Organic Usually applied to fertilisers which come from natural sources rather than pure (inorganic) chemicals.

Pan A hard layer of soil, usually just below the surface, caused by bad cultivation and insufficient aeration. Surface panning can be caused by excessive rolling and walking on the soil while it is too wet.

Perennial A plant that lives for many years and continues annually to flower and seed.

Pollination The transference of pollen from the male part of a flower to the female part of another – or, in some cases, the same – flower in order to cause fertilisation of seed.

Pricking out Transferring seedlings from pots or boxes, to larger pots or boxes or into prepared seed beds while they are so small that they have to be 'pricked' rather than planted into the soil.

Propagation The increase of plants by any means, seeds, layering, cuttings, division, grafting.

Pruning Cutting back a plant to produce a better shape or to increase fruitfulness.

Resting A plant making little or no growth, usually throughout winter, is said to be resting or dormant.

Root pruning The shortening, cutting or removal of roots, in order to decrease the vigour of a plant.

Runner A stolon or rooting stem such as is produced by strawberries. A means of propagating the plant.

Seed leaf The first leaf produced by a seed when it germinates. It usually differs in shape from the true leaves produced later.

Sour Applied to soils in a poor condition owing to lack of aeration or waterlogging. One in which the micro-organisms are not working properly.

Spit One spade's depth of soil.

Stopping The removal of the growing tip of a plant in order to make it branch out. Alternatively, in order to control the size and season of blooms.

Stratification Exposing certain seeds, usually those of trees or shrubs such as berries and hard-coated kinds, to frost. They should first be placed in pans, pots, or boxes between layers of sand.

Strike To root a cutting.

Taproot Technically, the first, usually unbranched, root made by a seedling. It is maintained by certain plants, in particular perennial weeds such as dandelion. Transplanting early prevents the formation of unwanted taproots in young plants and helps to create a good fibrous system of roots instead.

Tilth A fine crumbly texture produced by the soil after being tilled, usually by raking soil that has been left exposed to winter winds and frosts.

Topdressing The application of a food substance to the soil surface. Sometimes fresh soil is used.

Tuber A swollen root, such as anemone or dahlia, or a thickened underground stem which has buds or eyes, like a potato.

Weed A plant which grows where it is not wanted.

Winter wash A spray applied to deciduous, usually fruit, trees and bushes during winter when they are dormant.

Index

Abbreviation: d = line drawing